BUILDING A POSITIVE ATTITUDE

Rich Wilkins

Second Edition 1992

ISBN 0-9631968-1-2

Copyright © 1991 by Rich Wilkins.
This book may not be reproduced in any form, by any means, without permission in writing from the publisher.

Printed in U.S.A.

Attention corporations, sales groups, colleges, universities and other organizations:

This book may be purchased at bulk discount rates for use in educational programs, or as premiums in sales promotions or fund raising campaigns. For details contact: POSitive Publications, 4817 Running Fox Drive, Shepherdsville, Kentucky 40165 or telephone (502) 955-7269.

A GOLDEN ATTITUDE IS . . .

Always making today your best day

Taking pride in a job well done

Treating others with respect

Isolating your negative thoughts

Treating every new task as an opportunity

Utilizing your talents daily

Doing the job right the first time

Expecting positive outcomes daily

Speaking well of others everyday

ACKNOWLEDGEMENTS

This book would not have been possible without the inspiration and support of many people, some of whom I encountered even before I started my company. I want to thank my wife and children for the inspiration and support they have offered by letting me pursue my purpose to impact POSitively the attitudes of people around the world.

I also want to acknowledge and thank my secretary, Lois Bryan, for all the hard work and dedication she has brought to our company. She has entered each word of this book with enthusiasm and has made hundreds of changes to help bring it to perfection. Because of her dedication, loyalty, and patience, I am forever grateful. She also has been an outstanding example of what POSitive attitudes are all about.

Most of all, I want to thank those of you who are reading this book. Because of you, my purpose stays alive within me. And thanks to my good friend, Zig Ziglar, who has been telling people for years, "You are born for achievement, engineered for success and endowed with the seeds of greatness."

HOW TO GET THE MOST OUT OF THIS BOOK

Thank you for investing in this book to help you build POSitive attitudes toward yourself, others and success. The contents of my book are based on principles I have developed as a result of spending thousands of hours of training and speaking with people who are striving everyday to improve themselves. I have found that success starts with building a foundation of POSitive attitudes toward yourself and others.

Because we learn through repetition, I encourage you to read this book several times. The first time you read it, do it for the pleasure and enjoyment. Beginning the second time, as well as others to follow, underline important points, use a highlighter or make notes in the margin. Should you find a page that contains valuable information, simply turn down the corner to allow you to find it quickly. I especially encourage you to complete the exercises at the end of each chapter. Completing the exercises will increase your awareness levels of what you found to be important. Also, use this book as a tremendous resource for it's motivational sayings as well as ways to add energy and meaning to your company meetings.

This is my first book and the beginning of many more. I say this because there is so much to write about in regard to people understanding the tremendous potential they possess. Also in writing this book I have included a gift especially for you which can be found somewhere between the first and last pages — an idea or thought that has the possibility of POSitively changing your life. And remember your future is only as bright as your mind is open!

POSitively,

Rich Wilkins
"MR POS"

TABLE OF CONTENTS

CHAPTER 1
    ANATOMY OF AN ATTITUDE   13

CHAPTER 2
    BUILDING POSITIVE ATTITUDES
        TOWARD YOURSELF   19

CHAPTER 3
    BUILDING POSITIVE ATTITUDES
        TOWARD OTHERS   31

CHAPTER 4
    BUILDING POSITIVE ATTITUDES
        TOWARD SUCCESS   49

CHAPTER 5
    USING CREATIVE VISUALIZATION
        AND POSITIVE AFFIRMATIONS   65

CHAPTER 6
    POSITIVE MOTIVATIONAL SAYINGS   71

CHAPTER 7
    ENERGIZING YOUR COMPANY MEETINGS   121

CHAPTER 8
    HOW TO USE OUR GOLDEN ATTITUDE
        LAPEL PIN[SM] FOR MAXIMUM IMPACT   131

CHAPTER 9
  FIFTEEN WAYS TO USE OUR POSTERS
    AND PLAQUES TO POSitivelY IMPACT
    OTHERS AROUND YOU   137

CHAPTER 10
  PERSONAL AND PROFESSIONAL
    DEVELOPMENT RESOURCES   141

CHAPTER 11
  MOTIVATIONAL PRODUCTS   145

CHAPTER 12
  WORKSHOP INFORMATION   153

ORDERING INFORMATION   159

It's not your aptitude, but your attitude that determines your altitude in life.
                                    Zig Ziglar

CHAPTER 1

ANATOMY OF AN ATTITUDE

It was a fall afternoon when I found myself sitting on top of a large roll of carpet in an empty living room with people rushing about carrying furniture into the house. I can remember the day as clearly as if it were just yesterday — and it was 38 years ago. I was six years old. Until that time, I had lived with my father because my parents divorced when I was six months old. Then, suddenly, a decision had been made for me and my brother and sister to move into my mother's home. This was the day I found myself sitting on the large roll of carpet in the middle of my mother's living room wondering where I was, whose house I was in, and what plans had been made for the rest of my life. It was at this time that I made one of the most important decisions of my life. I decided that no one in the future would control my destiny. I was to trust no one but myself, and if I was going to make it in this world, it was going to be up to me. You see, this was the beginning of an attitude that I developed which played a significant role throughout my childhood and a large portion of my adult life. I was angered that someone else had made a decision that affected so much of my life without telling me. I'll bet you can relate to my story, and you probably have a similar story to share about yourself.

As time moved on, I began traveling through life with a very independent attitude. I did not allow anyone else to help me. I remember when I entered the University of Kentucky and was told by a career counselor that I probably would not make it through college because my ACT (college entrance exam) scores were too low. I recall saying under my breath, "You don't understand who I am. I am Mr. Independent and

I'm going to prove to you that no matter how dumb a standardized test score says I am, through my persistence and my independence I will make it through college," and I did. Five years later (not four) I was a graduate of the School of Business and had been married for one year. As my marital relationship progressed, my wife found me to be truly independent. By my fifth year out of college I had worked for three different companies. I required change.

I found that as we began to have a family, with two beautiful daughters, my relationships with them were very warm, tender and caring. However, there was a part of me that still would not turn loose of the independence and the hurt that I had felt as a six-year-old. Because of the independent attitude I had developed earlier in my life, my relationships with others were not complete. Thanks to my wife's love for me and our family as a unit, she has helped me work through my feelings to enable me to become a better spouse, father and speaker. After twenty-one years of marriage, and with my children becoming young adults, I feel that my life is at its peak. I am very thankful for being surrounded by people who love and care for me.

I am sharing this part of my story with you because I know that there are millions of other people in the world who can relate to how we develop early attitudes in our childhood years, especially those attitudes that impact feelings and belief systems towards ourselves, others and success in life. For me, life has now become fascinating; an adventure that brings new challenges and opportunities every day. I have also come to understand that one's attitude is not the beginning, but the end result of our thoughts. The beginning of the attitudes we have as adults are formulated, reinforced and finalized by our thoughts when we were children. The wonderful gift that has come to me as a speaker is that I understand that in educating and developing adults today, I am not dealing with *today's* issues, but the development of *yesterday's* attitudes. I see my job as being an inspirationalist with the objective of raising people's awareness levels about things that have occurred in their childhood in order to enable them to build better attitudes towards themselves, others and success. I believe that everyone has tremendous potential regardless of their age, shape, size, weight, color or aptitude. In this book I offer you basic principles you can use to discover the endless potential you possess.

First, let's look at how an attitude is developed. Most people think that new thinking is the result of a new attitude. Actually, their ATTITUDE is the result of NEW THINKING. That is, they must change their thinking first, before their attitude changes. There is a story about an inner-city school in New York City that was having a problem with a class of "high risk" students. Beginning the second semester of this particular school year, this class had been through four teachers, two of whom they had physically abused. The principal was in dire need of a teacher who could handle this challenging class. He could not find anyone except an elderly lady that they had to bring out of retirement to teach these high risk kids. As the retired teacher looked at the enrollment list she jumped out of her chair and said, "Yes, I would be more than glad to teach these gifted students." The principal exclaimed, "You don't understand, these are high risk students, not gifted students." "Obviously," she said, "you don't see what I do in these children." As she began building rapport with her students, they became role models in the school. They were not only well behaved, they also became some of the highest achievers within the school environment. At the end of the year the principal decided to have a banquet to honor this retired teacher to let her know how much he appreciated her extraordinary work. At the banquet her principal started honoring her by saying what a wonderful job she had done, that she was one of the world's best teachers, and she had accomplished things with her students that no one else could see possible. After about five minutes of praising her, she jumped up out of her chair and exclaimed, "Why Mr. Smith, I don't understand why you are giving me all the credit when it was actually your idea." Then he said, "I don't understand what you mean." She said, "Well it was your idea to put their IQ scores next to their names on the roster when you showed it to me." He laughed vigorously, and said, "I'm sorry, those weren't their IQ scores, those were their locker numbers!"

You see, it would appear that her attitude was the beginning of a difference that had a very POSitive impact on a number of people. However, before she could develop her "attitude of gratitude," she had to process her thinking, which in turn developed into her belief system (these are tremendously gifted students) which in turn, resulted in an attitude of encouragement. Most people in our world have this reversed. They think that attitude is the beginning of POSitive thinking. However, the attitude (which is what we see) is the result of the thought process repeating itself to the point of believability. The result of our belief system is our attitude. The diagram below will help you better understand what I am saying.

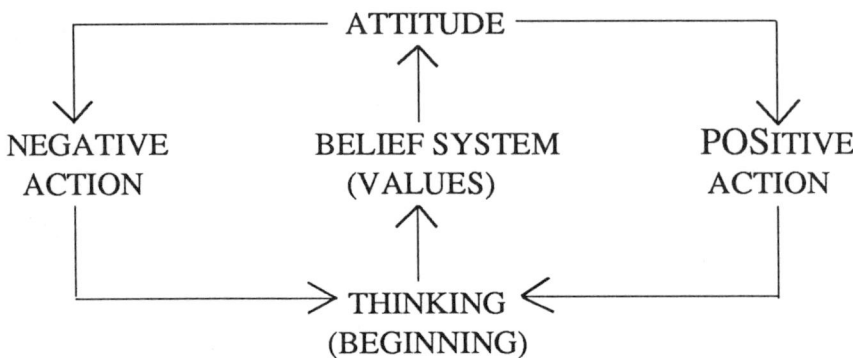

As the thought process takes on a negative or POSitive meaning and is repeated, it develops a cycle that is either POSitive or negative. In other words, negative thinking normally develops into negative attitudes which are reinforced through negative thinking and manifested again as negative attitudes. The same is true for the POSitive attitudes that we develop.

By the way, it is just as simple to develop POSitive attitudes as it is to develop negative attitudes, despite what you have been told. Because we live in a world in which our thinking usually is not challenged constructively on a daily basis, we aren't consciously aware of the attitudes we develop. Actually this is very simple. Let me demonstrate what I mean. Most of us are conditioned to think "we can't" instead of "we can" when presented with a problem (opportunity) as an adult. I'll prove this by asking you a very simple question. *By the time you were five years old how many times did you hear the word "NO?"* Hundreds of thousands of times, didn't you? Because our thinking and our attitudes are conditioned so well in our childhood, we unconditionally think "we can't" as we move into adulthood. We simply are more creative with our thinking as children because we haven't been conditioned to mediocrity.

A story was told about a semi-truck that was wedged under an overpass because it was too high. The city had all kinds of equipment on scene to free the semi-truck from the overpass. Several unsuccessful attempts to free the truck with a lot of "high tech" equipment had been made by the workers. A small boy on his bicycle wanted to offer a suggestion, but all of the adult workers were too busy to listen. One member of the fire department was sharing his pessimism about the situation with someone when the small boy walked up and said, "It looks quite easy to me. Why don't you let the air out of the tires and back it out from under the overpass?"

I hope that I have set the stage for us all to understand how our childhood experiences impact our belief systems as we grow into adults. We are who we are, and what we are, because of what has gone into our thoughts, which in turn built our belief systems and is recognized by others as our attitudes. With these thoughts in mind, I now want to help you further build POSitive attitudes towards yourself, others and success in the following chapters.

*Your future is only as bright
as your mind is open.*
                               Rich Wilkins

CHAPTER 2
BUILDING POSitive ATTITUDES
TOWARD YOURSELF

(You are the beginning of all POSitive change)

At the age of thirty, I began a new sales career with a large medical equipment company. I established myself as a very successful sales person and five years later was promoted into sales management. I also inherited a poorly performing sales region. I distinctly remember the Vice-President of Sales and Marketing telling me that he knew I could make a difference, that he had promoted the right man to bring this sales region to the number one sales position within the first year of my sales management career. My interpretation of his challenge was to bring my region to the number one spot no matter what the cost. By the end of the first year, guess what? Yes, I had brought my region from dead last to the number one position in less than a year.

One Sunday evening, my National Sales Director called and said he would like for me to be in the home office by noon the next day. That meant climbing aboard a plane and flying to St. Louis from Louisville. All kinds of visions were dancing through my head about all the praise and accolades I was to receive from our Vice-President of Sales and my National Sales Director. I couldn't wait to hear what an outstanding job I had done for my region because I had gotten the bottom line that was expected of me in my new position. As my National Sales Manager brought me into the Vice-President's office, I could tell that there was possibly another reason for my being there. My Vice-President started by saying how impressed he was with the sales results I had achieved within my region. However, he was very disturbed by the fact that I had lost three good sales people along the way, and the rest of my sales team was upset with my demands and unreasonable expectations. He informed me that getting results was important, but chasing away excellent sales people was not part of the plan. He asked me very bluntly if I felt I had a people problem, and I explained that up until this point I didn't think I did. He very succinctly gave me an option. He said, "If you feel like you have a problem with managing others, we will work with you in developing better skills to manage people. However, if you feel that you don't have a problem, I would like your resignation on my desk within three days." Needless to say, I was shocked! I will never forget how lonely my plane ride back to Louisville was that day.

My experience is what we commonly call a "significant emotional event" in one's life. It was at this point in my life that I decided that it was up to me to make a change about my attitude towards myself and how others viewed me. Quite frankly, not only will I never forget this event, I will never forget the importance of what my Vice-President of Sales and Marketing did for me. Yes, it's true, we can make a difference! POSitive change begins with you first, before you can expect to POSitively influence others.

In this chapter I will focus on four principles you can practice to build POSitive attitudes toward yourself. These principles are based on the experiences of thousands of people I have encountered through my personal, as well as professional life.

PRINCIPLE # 1

Believe in yourself!

A large part of becoming a better you is building a POSitive belief system about yourself. Most people go through life believing that they are not highly talented, and do not have tremendous potential. I view people as "diamonds in the rough" in which their total value lies inside themselves. However, we must peel off layers of distrust and negative experiences to get to our value, much like a diamond does not expose its beauty until it is discovered and polished. We become much more polished as we peel away the layers of negative programming from our childhood years.

In Mr. Cromwell's book entitled *Acres of Diamonds*, he tells a story about an African farmer who sells his farm to go prospecting for diamonds in other parts of North Africa. In his desperate search for diamonds away from his own farm, he dies frustrated and broke. However, the man who bought his farm one day was out in a stream and saw something glistening in its bed. As he picked up this crystal-like rock, he discovered that it was a diamond and, in fact, the largest diamond ever found in North Africa. We all have our own acres of diamonds within us! We simply need to recognize the value we have inside of us, begin believing it, polishing it, and sharing it with others.

In the seminars I conduct entitled "Building POSitive Attitudes Towards Yourself, Others and Success," I find that most people are confused about their competition. I can speak with any group of people and pose the question, "Who is your biggest competitor?" and they always wind up saying other people or companies. However, once you really think about it, *we* are actually our own biggest competitor. I say this because we have many tapes in our head that limit ourselves more than anyone else. Let me ask you one question that will prove my point again: "How many times did you heard the word 'no' by the time you were five years old?" Most people answer, "Hundreds of thousands of times." Recently a seminar participant jumped out of his chair and said, "I heard it millions of times. You didn't know my old man," he exclaimed. Well, I did, because I had a father who had a tendency to say no instead of yes most of the time. We become conditioned to negative programming by making statements to ourselves like:

> "I'm not really very smart."
> "I am too fat and people don't like me."
> "I can never remember names."
> "I never was very good in math."
> "I'll never be happy with my job."
> "I have to see it before I believe it."

The above statements are what I call "negative anchors." We anchor into thoughts and events constantly. The problem is that most of us anchor into negative thoughts (past failures) when we should be anchoring into POSitive thoughts (our successes) every day. Moving our thoughts and energy in the direction towards what we want to achieve makes all the difference. This process is what I call ANCHORING. This technique is very simple and all it requires is bringing your awareness levels up and changing your state of mind. Repeating the negative anchors in the previous paragraph is what most people do to bring negative results into reality for themselves. When you change your state of mind and your belief system to read:

"I really am smarter than I give myself credit for."
"I may be overweight, however, people do like me."
"I can remember names."
"I can become better in math when it becomes more important to me."
"I can be happy with my job."
"I do believe it and I am now seeing it."

Changing your state of mind is very important to give you the POSitive results that you desire. Each time you make a POSitive statement, anchor into that statement with your mental thought and visually relate the statement with yourself in some type of past successful activity.

I found it easy to eliminate my negative anchors by actually seeing myself positioned on the front of a boat. When I am feeling negative or I am nervous about accomplishing something, I picture myself standing on the front of a boat that is anchored, with its anchor rope in my hand. I pretend that my fear (negative anchor) is attached to the rope and I take a big pair of scissors and cut the rope to the anchor. As I cut it, I can hear it snap and feel my body begin to relax automatically. Next, I turn to a stack of positive anchors, grab one and concentrate on the POSitive thought the anchor represents. As I picture myself picking up the anchor, I repeat my POSitive thoughts as I swing it around and out into the water. I then tie it to the boat where I am standing to complete the anchoring event. This technique works well for me and is very empowering when I combine this with a prayer of thanksgiving. I will discuss prayers of thanksgiving more in the fourth principle of this chapter.

Some of us have been led to believe that to be highly confident, we border on being arrogant and too self-reliant. However, most athletes who perform extremely well are those persons who have tremendous self belief systems. Please keep in mind that your belief system is a product of your thoughts, and your attitude is a product of your belief system. Therefore, if you have POSitive thoughts about your own abilities and confidence levels, your attitudes toward yourself will build even more. Begin using POSitive anchors today and believe in yourself!

PRINCIPLE # 2

Focus on your successes and learn from your failures!

Three people that we read about in history that have failed probably more than anybody else are Thomas Edison, Babe Ruth and Walt Disney. However, we don't consider them failures! They learned from their failing events to become known as very successful people. Thomas Edison failed many thousands of times in his attempts to invent the electric light bulb. However, when asked by a young reporter prior to success how it felt to be a failure, he replied, "Son, you don't understand, I've never failed once. I have just found several thousand ways *not* to make an electric light bulb!" Most people would laugh at his response! However, he is right, because he had an attitude of determination, knowing that he would find the solution because he was learning from each one of his failing events. That's an attitude!

Babe Ruth struck out as much as any other player at bat in his era, but he was not known for his strike-outs, but for how powerfully he could hit the ball, and the number of times he hit it over the fence. Babe Ruth would swing at the ball so hard that often he would fall to his knees at the plate because of the power of his swing when he missed. Someone asked him one day how he handled the jeers of the crowd every time he struck out. He said it was easy, because he knew that the percentages were on his side. He was bound to hit a home run after a certain number of times at bat. This is also true for the successful sales person who understands that they have to hear a number of "nos" before they get a yes. Successful people focus on learning from their failures to become remembered by their successes. Walt Disney went broke seven times and had a complete nervous breakdown before he got Disneyland off the ground.

Too many people travel through life remembering and focusing primarily on their failures, which has a negative impact on their attitude toward themselves. Anytime we are focused on attempting something, such as achieving a goal, we will normally go through a certain number of failures before we achieve what we want. The important point is to stay focused on the event that you want to achieve successfully, not what you don't want. If you are a sales person, understand that you must go through a certain number of "no's" to achieve a successful sale with your prospect. Dr. Napoleon Hill says in his book, *Think and Grow Rich*, that people who become very successful in life, and have great attitudes towards themselves, are people who learn from adversity and defeat. It is with this in mind that he helps us understand the difference between a "big shot" and a "little shot." The only difference is that the big shot was once a little shot who kept on shooting!

My purpose in life is to impact the attitudes of people around the world. One of the goals I have established to support my purpose is to make 1,000,000 GOLDEN ATTITUDE LAPEL PINS℠ available by the end of 1994. Sure, I've gone through a series of failures in my attempts to make more attitude pins available, but I am focusing on my goal of 1,000,000 pins and developing programs to make that happen. I have been told by many people along the way that my goal is too aggressive and unrealistic. However, I keep focusing (visualizing) on my purpose like Thomas Edison and Babe Ruth did.

To begin to build even stronger and more POSitive attitudes toward yourself, take time to write up (not down) a success list. Write up all of the successes you feel good about. Write them on a 3" x 5" card and carry it with you every day and review them on a daily basis. When you feel like you have been defeated the most, and you feel that people are looking at you as a failure, get your success list out and review it. When you concentrate on your successes, you will again be reminded that you do have the ability and the talent to accomplish things you set out to accomplish. This change of thought allows you to let go of those negative anchors and develop POSitive anchors for yourself. But most of all, reminding yourself of your successes further builds a POSitive belief system in you. Remember what my friend Zig Ziglar says, "You are born for achievement, engineered for success and endowed with the seeds of greatness."

PRINCIPLE # 3

Surround yourself with POSitive people!

Building a POSitive world around yourself is simple, but it ain't easy! The reason I say this is because most people who are in your personal and business environment have been reinforced with negative thinking and negative events. We are scripted from our childhood to think NO instead of YES because, as you remember, we have heard the word NO hundreds of thousands of times by the time we are five years old. Also, we have heard the word DON'T and have looked up at the end of a big finger pointing at us many times as a child. If you are a parent or grandparent, try removing the word don't from your vocabulary when talking to your children or grandchildren. Talk to them in terms of what you want them to do, not what you don't want them to do.

Raise your awareness levels to understand the source of people's negativeness. I'm willing to bet that the majority of the conversations you encounter with others either begin with a negative statement, end with a negative statement, or involve a negative strategy. One of the hardest things to achieve when I became a POSitive person was to "cut the cord" in my relationships with others who were constantly negative. Many of your friends aren't even aware of their negative scripting and how they concentrate on negative outcomes because they rely on excuses instead of being solution-conscious. I am sure that you have encountered the "yes, but" person. This is the person who says they are interested in a solution. When you offer your opinion of the solution they come back with "yes, but . . . ." My rule of thumb is that when somebody comes to me with a problem and we begin brainstorming for a solution and when they use the "yes, but" statement with me three times, I politely excuse myself and move on to people who are interested in becoming solution-conscious and not obstacle-constructive. Simply surround yourself with people who have the same values, principles and thinking as you. There are many tremendously POSitive people in our world. Look for them and get to know them!

PRINCIPLE # 4

Have faith!

I can remember my first attempt at public speaking in a business environment. The opportunity came when I was to accept an award for the Outstanding Salesperson of the Year for my previous company. In a ten minute period of time, I managed to break every public speaking rule and look like a fool before an audience of about 125 sales people. I had to leave the podium and rush to the restroom to throw up because I was so nervous. It was at this time that I planted the seed in my subconscious mind that I wanted to become a professional speaker. As I began my journey for the next several years, I began utilizing a resource called prayer before each speaking event. In my earlier years as a professional speaker it sounded something like this: "Dear God, please give me the strength to get through this upcoming presentation as I am scared to death because I know the audience is more experienced than I am, and they are looking for new things for me to say. Please be by my side and help make my nervousness go away as I am very scared." I realized at the time that prayer was a source of empowerment that had the ability to help me through my nerve-racking experiences.

One day prior to a speech I was making before a large audience, I changed my prayer of desperation to a prayer of Thanksgiving. This is what it sounded like: "Dear Lord, thank you for this very successful presentation that I am about to make. My audience is caring, they want to see me succeed as a speaker, and I realize that all of my successes come solely through you. Once again, thank you for allowing me to make this very successful presentation and thank you for allowing me to remain on a positive path in life." Changing the attitude of my prayer from one of need, to one of Thanksgiving made all the difference. As a result, my speaking career took off!

As you begin to build POSitive attitudes toward yourself you will become aware of how important it is to become spiritually balanced in your life. *Your spiritual basis is the foundation for all of your successes and your motivation to learn from your failures.* Thanking your God on a daily basis for the most insignificant, as well as significant, events will take you to heights of building more POSitive relationships with yourself, others, success, and, most importantly, God. Take a minute right now and say a prayer of thanksgiving for something that has happened today. The "gift" in this exercise is also to think about your day to make you more aware of all the "mini" successes we all experience.

IN REVIEW

1. Remember to believe in yourself! You have tremendous potential and it is brought forward by telling yourself constantly that you have great potential. Build a belief system internally that says "I can" when others say "you can't." You can make a difference, and when you begin believing it you will see it! Cut the rope on your negative anchors and anchor into POSitive thoughts that build a better you.

2. Focus on your successes and learn from your failures. Begin your success list today by writing down five events that have happened in your life that you see as successes that make you feel good about yourself.

    1. _____
    2. _____
    3. _____
    4. _____
    5. _____

3. Remember to surround yourself with POSitive people and sever your ties with negative ones. Take this time to make a list of people whom you feel comfortable with, that share your values, and are interested in accomplishing things that are important to you.

    _____   _____
    _____   _____
    _____   _____

4. Remember to expand your spiritual base and thank God every day for all of the little things that help you to feel good about yourself. In fact, begin this process now by writing out a simple prayer of thanksgiving.

    _____
    _____
    _____

For a way to anchor our principles into your company, refer to our Golden Attitude Lapel Pin℠ and motivational plaques in the back of this book on pages 146 and 147.

*If you can see John Brown through John Brown's eyes,
you can sell John Brown what John Brown buys.*
                                                    Rich Wilkins

CHAPTER 3
BUILDING POSITIVE ATTITUDES TOWARD OTHERS

If you will recall my story earlier about how my sales people viewed me, keep in mind that before I could build POSitive attitudes toward others, I had to see a change in my attitude toward myself. Bob Conklin says in his book entitled, *How To Get People To Do Things*, you must first give others what they want; then they give you the things you want. Most people have that twisted around.

Conklin writes:

A man says to himself, "I would give my wife a box of candy if she would show me more affection."

An employer feels that an employee should get praise and recognition after putting forth some extra effort.

"I'll start having confidence in my kids when they get some decent grades in school," mutters a parent.

"I could get a lot warmer towards George if he weren't so cold and grouchy," Maude silently thinks.

A salesperson tells a sales manager, "Wow! would I ever be excited if I cracked the General Electric account!"

These people have the formula backwards.

The man has to bring his wife the candy first; then he will get more affection.

The employer must give praise and recognition first in order to bring forth the extra effort from the employee.

The parent has to express confidence in the kids first, then they will start coming through with better grades.

Maude has to warm up to George first; the indifference and grumpiness in George will melt away.

The sales person must generate excitement first, then the big juicy sales will fall into place.

So that's the way the law works. You first give others what they want; then they will give you what you want.

Robert Conklin brings out a good point about people. It's our responsibility first to decide to become solution-conscious with people. It is with this in mind that we'll look at four principles to help us build positive attitudes towards others.

PRINCIPLE #1

See John Brown through John Brown's eyes!

"If you can see John Brown through John Brown's eyes, you can sell John Brown what John Brown buys." Every good salesperson practices this integrity based principle because when you determine what is important to John Brown he will open up to you. It is with this principle in mind that we conduct our integrity sales training programs at the University of Louisville Sales School. Unfortunately, in expecting others to respond to us, we normally try to do things with them our way. As Bob Conklin reminds us, we must first see John Brown through John Brown's eyes to understand how to create value and give John Brown a reason to see things our way.

Seeing John Brown through John Brown's eyes means we have to take time to listen and ask questions to determine what is important. Normally, people will not open up for you until they trust you, so let's look at two main elements of any relationship.

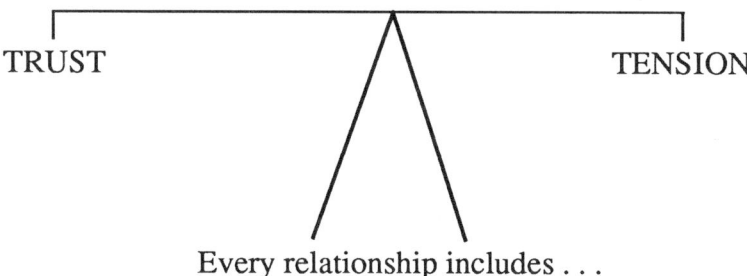

Every relationship includes . . .

As you can see from the above diagram, there is TRUST and TENSION in all relationships. They are directly related, which means when one goes up the other goes down. You will also find that trust and tension will be changing constantly throughout the relationship. Normally when we first meet someone tension is usually higher than trust because we don't know (trust) the person we are interacting with. As we develop the relationship in a POSitive manner, trust will begin to go up. However, you may ask a sensitive question of the person you are speaking with and the tension will rise. Also keep in mind that past experiences (both POSitive and negative) may be triggered which will cause trust and tension to fluctuate. Our goal should be to build trust with people when we are with them. Can you think of ways people build trust with you?

Seeing John Brown through John Brown's eyes (building trust) is not easy because generally we have a tendency to try to get people to see things our way first. However, if we will stop long enough to ask questions and listen, we can witness how much easier it is to build trust with others. Because people prefer for you to build trust with them their way, you will become aware of the four distinct styles of people we deal with on a daily basis. Let's look at my model of the four different styles of people on page 34. There are four factors we observe about people's styles. The first two

RELATIONSHIP ORIENTED

SUPPORTERS
(Consistency)

INITIATORS
(Influences)

STEADY ———————————————— IMPULSIVE

CONFORMERS
(Comply)

DOMINATORS
(Power)

TASK ORIENTED

are found at the top and bottom of the model with a vertical line between them; RELATIONSHIP-ORIENTED and TASK-ORIENTED.

We all fall somewhere on the vertical line. Some people are extremely relationship oriented and some of us are extremely task oriented. Relationship oriented people place a high value on relationships and are very friendly, warm, open, energetic and are great teamplayers. People are very important to them and they prefer getting results through people. On the other hand, task oriented people prefer to complete their task before they socially interact with people. They appear to be accurate, detail oriented, factual, results oriented and require a result in dealing with others. To build trust with Task Oriented people simply concentrate on the task at hand and give them results.

The next two factors we can observe about people's styles is how STEADY or IMPULSIVE they approach situations. People who are Impulsive have characteristics that may be observed as fast paced, reactive, aggressive, ego driven, opinionated and blunt. They also answer questions quickly without much hesitation and they react quickly to most situations. On the other hand, people who are steady have characteristics that may be observed as slow, methodical, processed, non-assertive and evenly paced. They have a tendency to pause at length before they answer your question. They require time because they are usually evaluating and processing information. To build trust with impulsive people simply pick up your pace and respond quickly to their requests. With steady people simply slow your pace down and give them time to respond.

Thus far we have been discussing four factors of people's styles. Now, let's take a look at each of the four styles to enable you to better see John Brown through John Brown's eyes. People who are relationship oriented and impulsive are referred to as INITIATORS. They have a tendency to control their environments by influencing the environment through initiating contacts with people. They may be seen by others as opinionated, assertive, blunt, loud, interactive, life of the party and initiate conversation with others. They talk about themselves a lot and are normally fast paced and make decisions quickly. They are also considered to be people-people. Can you think of anyone you know that is this style? Famous people who fall into the category of Initiators are Eddie Murphy, Johnny Carson and Joan Rivers. Professions that Initiators are attracted to are salespersons, public relations and professional actors.

People who are task-oriented and impulsive are referred to as DOMINATORS. They have a tendency to control their environment by dominating it and they influence others by dominating them. They may be seen by others as dominating, overbearing, demanding, overpowering, result oriented and somewhat insensitive. They are also fast paced and make decisions quickly, however, they have a tendency to make the decision thesmelves as opposed to asking others first. Do you know anyone that is this style? Famous people who fall into the category of Dominators are Clint Eastwood, Charles Bronson and Nancy of Charlie Brown. Professions that Dominators are attracted to are executive managers, Entrepreneurs and stock brokers.

People who are relationship oriented and steady are referred to as SUPPORTERS. They have a tendency to control their environment through steadiness and building trust by getting to know others personally. They may be seen by others as friendly, sincere, loyal, personable, warm, caring and into the relationship with others. They are also excellent listeners and very supportive of others. Famous people who fall into the category of Supporters are Mr. Rogers, Mary Tyle Moore and Mother Teresa. Professions that Supporters are attracted to are ministers, counselors and social workers.

People who are task oriented and steady are referred to as CONFORMERS. They have a tendency to control their environment by conforming to it and expecting the same of others. They are policy oriented people who expect things to be done by the book. They may be seen by others as analytical, accurate, cautious, withdrawn, unemotional and somewhat skeptical. They are excellent at setting policy and guidelines. Famous people who fall into the category of Conformers are Mr. Spock, Albert Einstein and Abraham Lincoln. Professions that Conformers are attracted to are accounting, engineering and data processing.

Each one of the four styles INITIATOR, DOMINATOR, SUPPORTER and CONFORMER accomplish tasks differently and at a different pace. This is why people have different attitudes and opinions of the same person because we have a tendency to see the world through our eyes, and not John Brown's eyes. Also people who are impulsive do not consider themselves blunt, over confident, opinionated or impatient.

However, oftentimes steady personalities will see them that way. Because people have different dominant styles they will experience personality conflicts and it usually occurs between opposite styles such as INITIATORS with CONFORMERS and DOMINATORS with SUPPORTERS. If you are married or have a companion, research shows that you probably have a relationship with someone of the opposite style. This is found to be true because of the universal law, "opposites attract." Opposite styles also account for many of the arguments we witness among others. If you want to build POSitive attitudes towards others, take time to see John Brown through John Brown's eyes. As you begin to better understand how others like to develop relationships and perform tasks, you will be able to work with them on a much more harmonious basis both personally and professionally. As we "flex" from our styles to meet other's styles on a mutually beneficial basis, we will build trust with others and see John Brown through John Brown's eyes. This concept is empowering for raising your own awareness levels about yourself, as well as how you see others. Should you want to learn more about this concept call our office (502-955-7269 or FAX 502-955-9795) to inquire about having us conduct a seminar in your company or for information about our public seminars we conduct in Louisville, Kentucky. Also, should you want a ten page Styles Report sent to you for a cost of only $30 ($100 value) because you have invested in this book, simply complete the questionnaire in the back of this book on page 152. I have personally taken over ten thousand people through our seminars and questionnaires with companies such as Citibank, Ford Motor Company, Atlas Van Lines and many others.

PRINCIPLE #2

Don't compete with others — inspire them.

We live in a world of competition, and it begins at a very early age. We compete as babies to cry loud enough to get mother's or father's attention to get our diaper changed, a nice warm bottle of milk, or simply to get enough attention to feel important. As we become slightly older, we are competing with mother and father to get their attention while they are reading the newspaper, watching TV or talking with their friends.

While sitting in our pediatrician's office with my youngest daughter, I watched the game of competition begin as several young children entered the waiting room and eyed the world's most popular toy in the middle of the room. It was obvious that the first child to the toy became its momentary owner until it was ripped out of his or her hands by another child. This act alone heightens competition to a degree that can become very destructive to building POSitive attitudes with others in their present environment and more importantly in the future.

As you can see, we are scripted to compete with others in our personal lives, business lives, and even our spiritual lives. It seems to be the thing to do. It gives us the impression that we are better than others when we are temporarily "king of the mountain" — until someone comes along and crushes our realty. Fortunately, through my own experiences in life, I have learned that as I begin to compare myself to others in achieving excellence, I not only don't perform as well, I don't feel as good about myself. As a member of Toastmasters International, I have participated in several speech contests in which everyone who participates begins to worry and fret about other contestants' reputations as speakers in their attempt to win the contest. When I finally learned not to worry about others' strengths and focus on my own abilities and HONE them into skills of excellence, I became very proficient at the speech-making process. People who are interested in building POSitive attitudes towards others do not compete. What they prefer to concentrate on is their own skills, inspiring others to achieve their own level of performance. Unfortunately, most people do not understand how we have been scripted through our childhood years to become extremely competitive adults in all aspects of our lives. This competition is responsible for poor self-esteem, poor self-image, and volatile relationships in our personal and professional lives.

There is a story told of a young man who participated in a Special Olympics quarter-mile race. He went into the race being told that what is important is to come out on top, by being the first one to run across the finish line. As the gun went off at the starting line, they all left from the same position and began their competition around the track. As Billy rounded the last corner of the race, his very best friend tripped on his heel and stumbled to the ground. Momentarily Billy turned his head to see his friend come crashing to the ground and burst into tears. Billy hesitated, as he was torn between competing with his friend or helping him. Almost instantaneously he made his decision to run back to where his friend lay on the track, help him up, and then cross the finish line together. Although they weren't the first over the finish line, they were the first in many people's hearts that day. They helped many people understand what life is really about . . . that it is not competing with others, but striving to inspire others.

PRINCIPLE #3

Become a good finder

The most exciting thing about building POSitive attitudes towards others and having them respond to you is that it all starts with you. You are the beginning of all positive change. It seems that we live in a world where we are always looking for the imperfections in others. By the way, this is also a scripting process that is left over from childhood. We as parents have a tendency to look for perfection in our children. I can think of two examples that brought this point home to me. My first realization was when my oldest daughter was in middle school and she brought home a report card that showed all A's and one B. You got it! I thought how great her report card was, but . . . why did she get one B? I seemed to focus on the B by asking why it couldn't have been an A. I took an outstanding report card and made our daughter feel like she had really messed up because she had a B.

A second example is one that a lot of us do, especially we fathers, to our children without realizing it until later in life. During a conversation with my oldest daughter, I realized how much I had negatively impacted her thinking. When she was a small child I was very busy traveling and building my corporate career. Our yard was very large and our grass needed to be cut routinely and with perfection. I always cut our grass with the same preciseness and perfection as I expect from myself as a professional businessman. Laura would appear outside wanting to ride with me on the lawn tractor. I would put her up on my lap and we would take off down the side of our front yard in high gear with my goal of cutting the grass so impeccably that all of my neighbors could see a master craftsman at work. Because it was the fatherly thing to do, I would let Laura steer the tractor while we were cutting the grass. However, she never cut the rows as straight as I wanted, and I would wind up grabbing the wheel, getting the tractor back on track and exclaiming to her how important it was to cut the rows straight. I can remember how she would look at me somewhat confused, as she thought it was supposed to be fun to be on a lawn tractor with her father on a Saturday. However, it was another task to me, and the end result was perfection, not enjoyment with my daughter. Fortunately, several years later we got into a discussion about our old house and the grass cutting routine. My daughter looked at me and said, "You know Dad, I never understood why the grass had to be cut so perfectly and I always wound up with my feelings hurt and disappointed because it was not a fun experience." I feel fortunate that she brought that to my attention so that we could discuss it. I could absolve myself for being responsible for some of her negative feelings about the event we both experienced earlier in her childhood. Laura is an outstanding daughter and the last thing I wanted to do was to negatively impact her the way I did. However, it seems that we get so caught up in the hustle-bustle of everyday living that we lose sight of the fact that people should *always* be more important than events and accomplishments along the way.

We need to be more conscientious of becoming good finders with others. Good finders are people who see goodness in others without even looking for their imperfections. When it comes to relationships, I think one of the best "good finders" I have seen in my lifetime is my wife, Nan. She has such a natural style of looking for the good in others and complimenting them in a very POSitive fashion that makes them feel good. Frequently she will be in a discussion with someone who is finding imperfections in someone else and Nan will consistently look for the qualities that build this person up, not down.

Take some time to go through an exercise to write down the good qualities of people you encounter in your daily lives. If you have a spouse, companion or children, take a minute during the day to write down those

POSitive qualities that you see in them. They are there and they are terrific! However, we have a habit of looking for the bad things. This is because we are constantly being bombarded by others who are looking at the imperfect way that we do things, and always pointing out our shortcomings. Become a good finder of others and witness the POSitive feeling it brings back to you. The return that you receive is how good it makes you feel.

PRINCIPLE #4

Go the extra mile for others

When our two daughters were very young, my wife decided to attend an out-of-town convention for a week. As she shared her excitement with me about attending this convention, I said I thought it would be a great idea and I would take a vacation and stay at home with our two daughters.

As I mentally prepared for our week together, I began to envision myself as the perfect "Mr. Mom." About mid-afternoon on Sunday we took my wife to the airport, gave her plenty of hugs and kisses, and waved very energetically through the glass windows as she boarded her plane. She was excited about going to the convention and we were excited about being at home for a week of adventures. Being the typical father, I began asking them to set priorities which started with our evening meal. It was unanimous, we all wanted to eat at Kentucky Fried Chicken; but we were to take it home where we could be messy and just act crazy. We swung by Kentucky Fried Chicken, ordered a couple of chicken snacks with all white meat, extra mashed potatoes and gravy, and my favorite, a chicken liver dinner. As I picked up my order, I momentarily thought, "Should I check the order to make sure it is correct?" No, it wasn't necessary because I was sure that they had filled the order properly. Off we went headed towards home to enjoy what we had been waiting for all afternoon.

Upon sitting down at the kitchen table and unpacking our order, I discovered that our counter person had filled our order incorrectly. We were famished, ready to eat, and discovered we had dark pieces of chicken instead of white pieces; they had forgotten one of the orders of mashed potatoes; and my livers were not hot. Needless to say, I wasn't very impressed with the quality of service. Because my children were preschool age at the time, I could not leave them at home and go back and have the order filled correctly. I had to pack up the kids and drive back to Kentucky Fried Chicken. As I approached the counter, the person who had filled my order was about to wait on me again. I laid the order on the counter and she said, "Sir, can I help you?" I said, "No, you've already tried to help me. I would like to talk with your store manager." She said, "Well, if you have a problem, I'll take care of it." I responded impatiently by saying, "No, you've done enough for today. I prefer to talk to your manager." About one minute later the store manager appeared. He was a very young man who looked like he didn't have enough experience himself to fill an order, let alone manage others. I started into the manager and impatiently informed him that obviously whoever filled my order could not read because it says right on my cash register receipt what I had ordered. If he would check my order he would become aware that it was filled incorrectly and very inconsiderately.

As I shared my story with him, I could feel myself becoming even more angered because I just knew that this person would blame his employee's inadequacies on something else. As I unloaded on this young man he stood there patiently and listened to what I had to say. When I finally shut up, what I heard him say stuck with me for a long time. I have shared it with many audiences across the country. He looked me comfortably in the eye and said, "Sir, I'm very sorry and I understand how you must feel. Recently we have had some trouble with the person that filled your order and we are working with her to help her understand the importance of filling orders correctly." "Mr. Wilkins," he said, "if you have a few minutes I would like to completely refill your order, and by the way, what type of soft drink do you and your daughters like?" I responded by saying I preferred diet drinks and my children preferred regular drinks. He said, "Why don't I get you a soft drink while we are refilling your order." I was pleasantly surprised by his responsiveness to our dilemma.

Within three minutes he appeared with our correct order and he apologized in depth for the delay and inconvenience. He had responded in a very POSitive manner and he helped me understand that day the real meaning of going the extra mile for others. He looked at me again and said, "Mr. Wilkins, not only would I like to return your order to you correctly, I would like also to totally refund the purchase price of your order." Now, what do you suppose I said to this? I responded by saying, "Oh, that's all right, I simply expect you to fill the order correctly and you don't need to return my money." He insisted that he would like to refund my investment as it wasn't the cost of the order that was important, it was establishing and maintaining a happy business relationship. He went the extra mile!

I have shared this story with thousands of people to help them understand how important it is for all of us to consider going the extra mile for others. By the time this young manager had finished POSitively responding to me, I had the greatest respect for his awareness level about people. Not only that, I've been back numerous times for more food.

How often are you going the extra mile for others in your business and personal life? We are scripted through childhood events not to consider going out of our way for others without considering the attitude, "What's in it for me if I do this for you?" Napoleon Hill writes in his book *Think and Grow Rich* that those who go the extra mile for others will reap many rewards in life. To understand the value of this concept we must place others in the #1 position and us in the #2 position. We have to develop the attitude that says, "I'm going to do this for others unconditionally because of how good it makes me feel inside."

Take this opportunity to make a list of how you've gone the extra mile for others, and as you complete the list, reflect back on how it made you feel. If you hold the door open for someone else expecting them to say "thank you," you'll probably set yourself up for disappointment. However, if you hold the door open because it makes you feel good to go the extra mile for somebody else, you will come out feeling on top of the world. It's the mind set, and the attitude that you develop towards serving others that makes the difference.

I have talked to a lot of people in the business world about how they effectively manage others. One of the most knowledgeable, as well as a good friend of mine, is a Management Professor at the University of Louisville School of Business. His name is Dr. Lyle Sussman and he has helped me further understand the intricacies of how to manage and motivate others. He has recently authored a book entitled *Smart Moves,* which is one of the most effective books I have read for people who are in management and leadership positions with their companies. Should you want to contact Dr. Lyle Sussman, his associate Sam Deep or inquire about ordering his book, you may reach him at (412) 487-2379.

IN REVIEW

Let's take a minute to review the four principles we discussed to build POSitive attitudes towards others.

1. SEE JOHN BROWN THROUGH JOHN BROWN'S EYES — Keep in mind that there are four different styles of people that we interact with on a daily basis. The only way that we can build value for them and heighten our attitudes is to see the world through their eyes. This principle is very simple. It requires getting to know others' thoughts, feelings and values. Before you tell someone else they are right or wrong, spend a short period of time trying to see the issue through their eyes.

2. DON'T COMPETE WITH OTHERS — INSPIRE THEM — Remember that we are scripted very heavily as young children to compete with others all the time. We have a tendency to go through life trying to do better, achieve more, and elevate ourselves above others. Take some time to think about how you can get out of this thing called "competition" in relationships and begin to inspire them through developing value for them. Should you be placed in a situation, whether it be in your job or in your personal life, to compete with others, simply focus on what you do best and try to be an inspiration to others in the process. Should you win at something, don't make it sound like you are the best. Turn around and support POSitive things you saw others do in the process. Inspire them to higher levels of confidence in their own abilities and talents.

3. BECOME A GOOD FINDER — As adults, we have a tendency to be very critical of others around us. Change your way of thinking by becoming a good finder in others. Look for those things you feel are POSitive characteristics that they exhibit. If they have a tendency to think negatively about most outcomes, be supportive by helping them understand that it's as easy to

focus on POSitive outcomes as it is negative ones. If you are a parent or grandparent and you are faced with the report card issue that we were as parents, don't concentrate on the one bad grade. Concentrate on the good grades they have achieved. If you are a child, teenager or young adult, concentrate on the good things that you see in people who are older than you. Break out of your negative scripting of being critical about others. Go out and develop a better relationship with someone else; get out a sheet of paper and list all of the POSitive points that you see in them instead of focusing on the negative ones.

4. GO THE EXTRA MILE FOR OTHERS — This is a grand "universal" principle that is very powerful in building attitudes towards yourself and others. When you see people who constantly go the extra mile for others, you'll find that they are more content with themselves and have excellent relationships with other people. However, remember how we have been scripted in our early childhood years to do only enough to get by. We have a tendency to look always for short cuts and, unfortunately, to short change ourselves and others. The next time you are in a fast food restaurant, clean up your own table and someone else's, even though it is not expected of you. Make sure that you give extra value back to other people by making it a habit to do more than what is expected. If you want more salary in your job, constantly go the extra mile in your work environment. If you want a better relationship with your spouse, constantly take the responsibility of going the extra mile. If you are a child and want more allowance from your parents, constantly go the extra mile and watch what happens. Many great gifts in life are available to all of us when we simply open ourselves up. If you want to achieve a #1 position in life, you are first going to have to place yourself in the #2 position, and be of service to others.

*The biggest mistake a person can make
is to be afraid of making one.*
                                M. J. Babcock

CHAPTER 4
BUILDING POSITIVE ATTITUDES
TOWARD SUCCESS

I was born in Mount Clemens, Michigan, in the parking lot of St. Joseph's Hospital (we didn't make it to the hospital on time). My parents divorced soon after my birth, and my brother, my sister and I quickly became products of a broken home. My parents were heavy drinkers and smoked about three packs of cigarettes a day. I distinguished myself in elementary school by getting caught stealing balloons from my kindergarten teacher's desk drawer. I soon learned that I didn't like school and I struggled to make it to the fourth grade. It was at this year that my teacher decided that I wasn't smart enough to continue to the fifth grade and I was held back a year. By the time I was ten years old, I had been manipulated, rejected, made fun of, and physically and sexually abused by my older brother. By the time I was twelve, both of my parents had remarried and divorced for a second time. By the time I was sixteen, I was so short I had to sit on two telephone books to see over the car steering wheel when taking my driver's test (I felt like a failure). Because I felt so insecure about myself, I became a troublemaker and had to move to Kentucky with my father. As I entered the University of Kentucky, my counselor told me that I had scored so poorly on my college entrance exam that he was convinced I would never finish college. My senior year in college I married my wife, Nan, and I saw in her what I never had in my family — security. She went the extra mile constantly by looking for the good things about me that no one else had. She accepted me for what I was and encouraged me every day. Together we are the proud parents of two beautiful daughters, Laura and Erin, who are living proof that miracles do happen.

I have been through several very successful careers and as I write this book, I am in the process of fulfilling my life's overall purpose of positively impacting the attitudes of people around the world. I currently own my own company, live in a beautiful home, and most importantly am surrounded by people who care for me. *I have gone from feeling like a failure as a child to seeing myself as a successful adult.* **If I can be successful, you can too!** As I look back on what I have enabled myself to do throughout my years of negative programming, I've become very aware of how important it is for our awareness levels about ourselves to increase before we can bring about change. I also fully understand now that success must begin with me. I recently heard Wayne Dyer say, "Successful people become successful because they first feel success from within." As my friend, Zig Zigler, says, "You are born to achieve, engineered for success, and most importantly, endowed with the seeds of greatness."

In this chapter I want to discuss the three principles I have become aware of in the last two years that have brought me wealth, health and success. These are my gifts to you. Should you decide to develop and practice these principles, you will find that you too can have anything in life you want if you help enough other people get what they want.

PRINCIPLE #1

Have definiteness of purpose

When my daughter Laura was in middle school, she announced one day that she wanted to be the field commander of her band when she entered the eighth grade. As she conveyed this idea to our family, she became excited, and we became excited for her. When she went to school the next day she shared her news with her friends which in turn created higher energy levels. As she started to share her enthusiasm with her band director, she heard something that I had been hearing the majority of my life. Her band director responded by saying, "Oh Laura, you are too short to be a field commander!" Needless to say, she was somewhat frustrated by her band director's comment. However, she began disregarding what other people said she was capable of doing and developed her PURPOSE to become a leader in her band. Through a lot of focused thinking, re-affirming and visualizing, she became the field commander of her band in the eighth grade. She learned very early in life the power of developing a clear purpose. By the way, she also became the field commander of her high school band as a senior, and is the only one in the history of her high school to have received the first place competition award for field commander. Not bad, for someone being told four years earlier that she was too short to be a field commander!

It's my conviction that if you build POSitive attitudes towards yourself and others, success is semi-automatic! However, keep in mind that all change begins with you first. You chart your own course to success or failure. Most people don't achieve high levels of success because they are not clear in their thinking as to what they want to be, or to accomplish, or what they want to do at some future point in time. The most powerful principle I have found in the success process is developing your definite purpose.

I want to make sure that we understand clearly how developing a purpose is different from setting goals. A purpose is a strategic idea, concept or belief system that someone develops clearly, and are emotionally attached to. Actually it is a reflection of your values. My purpose, for example, is to POSitively impact the attitudes of people around the world for the rest of my life. Your purpose should be kept as simple as possible and involve the betterment of people. With these two ideas in mind, you will be amazed at what you can accomplish with a clear purpose.

Goals, on the other hand, are something that we strive to achieve over a period of time. The problem with only setting goals and not having a definite purpose is that many people establish multiple goals that are not a reflection of their values. When we do this without a clear purpose, we become fragmented with our activities. This is very frustrating. I am sure you can relate to what I am saying. *Also, your goal achievement should become the structure for fulfilling your purpose.* I will give you an example of what I am talking about. The two goals that I have established to accomplish my purpose are to make available 1,000,000 GOLDEN ATTITUDE LAPEL PINS[SM] in the next five years, and to become one of the top ten speakers in this country in the next ten years. (For a description of our GOLDEN ATTITUDE LAPEL PIN℠ see pages 131 and 146.) I only have two goals and by focusing on these, I will fulfill my purpose. All of my daily business activities fall within the parameters of my purpose. When I fulfill my purpose, I will move on to another purpose that is important to me and is also a reflection of my values.

Let's look again at Thomas Edison, Babe Ruth and Walt Disney. They were able to continue through their failing events because they had a clear purpose. Thomas Edison's purpose was not to invent the electric light bulb! His purpose was to improve the quality of life of people in the world. He fulfilled his purpose by completing his inventions, one of which was the electric light bulb. His inventions became his goals. Walt Disney's purpose was to bring creativity and animation to our world. His goals were Disneyland, and Disney movies. Babe Ruth's purpose was to make a name for himself in baseball, and he did that by hitting a great many home runs (his goal). Because their purposes were clear and in place, they were filled with desire and went after their goals with enthusiasm and persistence. Desire, enthusiasm and persistence are automatic when you are "sold" on your purpose.

In our seminar entitled "Building POSitive Attitudes Towards Yourself, Others and Success," we help people begin the process of developing their purpose. Establishing one's purpose takes focused thinking and concentration. Your purpose is not always crystal clear, but it becomes clearer as time passes and you think more about what is important to you. Also, as Napoleon Hill states, "As your purpose becomes clearer, you develop more desire and you become more enthusiastic and persistent in your pursuit of success." Having a clear purpose will enable you to become a "meaningful specific" and can remove you from the ranks of the "wandering generalities!"

Most people who are good at what they do develop a subconscious or unaware purpose as they improve themselves. If you are in sales, your current need may be to make lots of money. However, should you transform your present need into developing a purpose to determine and fill the needs of your prospects on a daily basis, watch what happens! Two goals you may establish to fulfill your purpose are: 1) Become a more effective listener. 2) Ask more effective questions. If you are a professional manager, your purpose may be to help others grow on a daily basis. Two goals you may establish for yourself are: 1) Attend three effective management seminars in the next year. 2) Develop a feedback system that people can use to communicate with you more effectively in the evaluation process. If you are a teacher (who are very important persons to me since they spend as much time with my children as I do), your purpose may be to improve the quality of life with your students when they are with you in school. A couple of goals you may establish to help you fulfill your purpose are: 1) Become a good "finder" with your students. 2) Make it a daily practice to go the extra mile.

Determining your purpose begins with:

1. Thinking about what is important to you in your personal, business and spiritual life.
2. Writing out your purpose statement on a sheet of paper.
3. Recognizing your feelings about your purpose.
4. Establishing two or three goals for your purpose.
5. Becoming persistent about your purpose in the face of temporary setbacks and rejection.

I envision my purpose to be like the roof of a building pointed upward in the middle, and my goals are the four walls that support it. For optimum achievement, you must develop goals that fall in line with your purpose. As Dr. Napoleon Hill says, "If you can conceive it and believe it, you can and will achieve it."

PRINCIPLE #2

Seeing failure as a stepping stone to success

In Dr. Robert Schuller's book entitled *Success is Never Ending, Failure is Never Final* he asks this question: "What great thing in life would you attempt if you knew it was impossible to fail?" What a terrific question! We learn at a very early stage of our childhood how embarrassing and painful it is to fail. We hear the word failure many times every day and we compete with others to a point where someone has to lose. Failing is a tremendous part of everyone's life and happens more frequently in most successful people's lives. How many times we fail is not important; learning from the failing experience is important.

In my many years of dealing with people, I have found that their big fear is failure. We have been criticized thousands of times as children and adults for attempting something that didn't work out. So it seems almost natural that we avoid trying things because of two events in life — failure and success! Because we have been criticized as we grew up, our fear of failure is very strong. We are forced to compete with others and there is more humiliation and self-doubt as we experience failing events. As we grow into adults, we develop strong fears of success. Yes, that's right, we have a fear of success! I became aware of this as a sales manager early in my career. Sales people would actually diminish their production the last quarter of the year. When I asked why they were slacking off, they would reply, "If I blow the numbers out this year, you and the company will expect a lot more from me next year." Also, I would hear, "Because I was number one this year, I'm sure you expect that of me again next year."

Some students don't make straight A's in school (even though they are capable) because they know that once they do they are expected to repeat it. Some teachers don't strive to become "teacher of the year" because of what is expected afterwards. The list goes on and on. Successful people confront their fear of success and understand that they are their own biggest competitor. Yes, we are our own biggest competitor!

As a member of Toastmasters International, I have been a speech contestant in many events. When I focus on perfecting my speech for myself and my audience, I normally perform very well and win speech-making awards. However, when I get caught up in thinking of other people in the contest as competitors, I normally don't perform as well.

Let me demonstrate how we are our biggest competitor. In the diagram below I would like you to connect all the dots with four straight lines without taking your pen off the page. To repeat: Take your pen or pencil and see if you can connect all of the dots with four straight lines without taking your pen off the paper.

```
•        •        •


•        •        •


•        •        •
```

Let me help you with the solution to this problem (opportunity). If you are an adult, you have probably been conditioned not to see the solution. We are conditioned to see things a certain way because of our experiences in life. In helping you to solve this problem, what *figure* do you visualize when you see the nine dots? Most people see a square. If you do also, you have just limited yourself and will not come up with the solution. However, as I said before, because we compete against ourselves by imposing limitations, we normally want to stay within the square that we visualize. By the way, most younger children can see the solution to this very easily. They are not yet conditioned to see things in a fixed way. Most adults look for the solution inside the square. However, the solution to our problem requires us to go beyond our self-imposed limitations (outside of the square as shown on the next page).

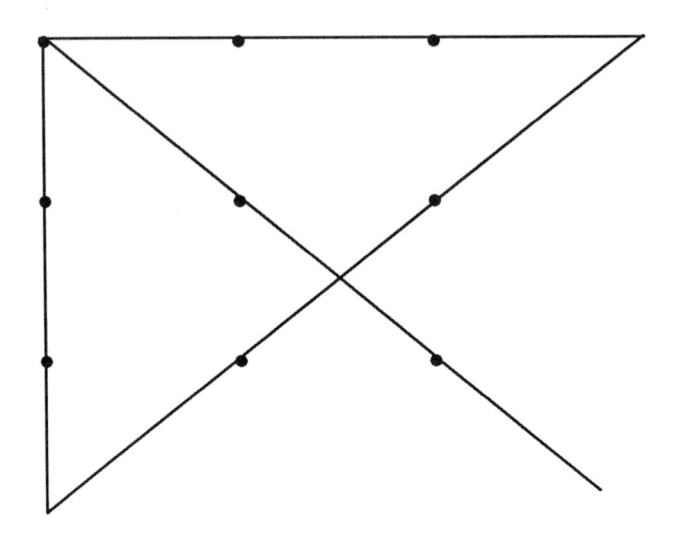

On a daily basis we impose limitations on ourselves. Here are some examples:

1. We don't give ourselves credit for our own valuable thoughts.
2. We tell ourselves that we are not good in various areas such as math, spelling, talking to others, etc.
3. We think "I can't" before we think "I can."
4. We live daily for other's approval.
5. We simply give up too early on our daily challenges.
6. We don't include others in attempting to solve our problems.

I know that you can relate to how we limit ourselves more than others limit us. We beat ourselves up mentally more than anyone else, and we pull ourselves back physically more than anyone else. Become more active with your POSitive thinking by convincing yourself that you "can" before you think you "can't." Forget about being criticized by others because you may not achieve your goal, and instead, set your meaningful goal with the confidence that you can achieve it . . . and should you not achieve your goal, have you anything to lose? Absolutely not!

Learning from failure is one of the greatest gifts we can give ourselves. As you are challenged on a daily basis to achieve your goals, keep in mind how important it is to learn from your experiences in the process. Focus on the outcome that you want, and develop the attitude that you will achieve it over a period of time. When something goes wrong, don't ask why, simply determine what happened and learn from it to become a better person. As Dr. Robert Schuller says, "Tough times don't last, tough people do." It's simply a matter of time in learning how you can approach your challenge from a different perspective to get the result that you want. Always look at your failures as stepping-stones to success and not as obstacles... and remember that your future is only as bright as your mind is open!

PRINCIPLE #3

Serve others

Recently I was to conduct a motivational program for an out-of-town company. I had booked my airline tickets with my travel agent and as I walked up to the ticket counter to give my ticket to the agent, I encountered a person who was giving the ticket agent a very difficult time. She apparently didn't understand why her ticket was scheduled the way it was. The agent she was dealing with so negatively obviously had nothing to do with her travel itinerary. As I stepped up to the counter I caught the agent's name and greeted him with POSitiveness and empathy. I said, "Earl, how are you doing today?" He literally stepped back from the counter, glanced at my ticket, looked up and said, "Mr. Wilkins, I'm doing fine and it's good to see you again." What's interesting is that I had never met Earl before in my life, but because I responded to him POSitively and used his first name, he thought he should know me. We immediately began to carry on an upbeat conversation, and he said,"Mr. Wilkins, I'm sure you have a Gold Card for our Frequent Flyer Program don't you?" I said, "Earl, I don't, because I haven't flown on TWA for quite some time. In fact, I don't even have my bonus coupons with me."

He responded by replying that that was no problem and he would fix me up in the computer. Within the next two minutes he said, "By the way, we have a fairly light schedule today so I'm sure you wouldn't mind if I just upgraded you to first class, would you?" I responded appropriately and thanked him very much. As he was updating my ticket, he responded again by saying, "Well what the heck, we might as well leave you in first class on the way back too."

Now, I am convinced that Earl gave me extra value on my flight simply because I gave him extra value in my approach and initial relationship with him. There is a Universal Law that says, when you put yourself in a serving role and give others value unconditionally, the value will return to you. We may not always recognize what is returned, or when, but it will come back to you. Earl's way of returning it to me was by upgrading my flight that day from coach to first class. There are three ideas you can practice to impact your success with others on a daily basis.

1. USE THE PERSON'S NAME YOU ARE INTERACTING WITH. The sweetest sound for anyone to hear is their name. If you will "dust" the conversation with the person's name you are interacting with, you will find that they will respond to you very POSitively. People like to hear their name used in a POSitive fashion with a comfortable voice tone. While recently conducting training for a local bank, we were discussing the importance of using customers' names. One of the participants objected because she felt that she might mispronounce a customer's name. However, you have nothing to lose if you are not sure how to pronounce someone's name. Simply ask them! This small principle alone will draw you into POSitive conversation and build POSitive attitudes with others.

2. SMILE! Yes, smile at people when you are talking with them. A smile on your face triggers POSitive emotions within you and also transfers those emotions to the person you are smiling at. Keep your smile comfortable and intermittent throughout your conversation, and smile slightly at

the beginning of each sentence and as you respond to them. Smiling with others is one of the small miracles we witness in life. Watch what happens the next time you look at somebody and smile. I will assure you that 99 out of 100 times you will get a smile back which will cause you to feel better about yourself and the person receiving your warm smile.

3. MAKE COMFORTABLE EYE CONTACT WITH OTHERS. Eye contact is one of the strongest means of communication with people. If you are a parent, you can use it to send both POSitive and negative messages to your children. If you are a child or young adult, you can also use comfortable eye contact with your parents to get a more favorable response from them. People like it when you look them in the eye as you talk to them. Make it a point to make comfortable, intermittent eye contact throughout your conversation with others. Watch how they respond! Another benefit of making eye contact with others is that it is a means of building trust. Most people will tell you they don't trust people who can't look them in the eye. So, eye contact is the vehicle that will bring a POSitive response from those that you are interacting with.

4. SAY "THANK YOU" A LOT. Let me say that one more time. SAY "THANK YOU" A LOT! Thanking people for things they do for you in your professional and personal life is a way of getting them to respond to you. It is evidence of putting yourself in a serving role to them. We don't hear enough "thank yous" from people on a daily basis. However, there is a secret to understanding how saying thank you can help you feel better inside about yourself. The next time you hold the door open for someone else expecting them to say thank you, you may set yourself up for disappointment big time. However, if you hold the door open for them because it makes you feel good, that's what makes the difference when you put yourself in a serving role to others, because it

makes you feel good about yourself. As you feel better about yourself, you'll also feel better about others, and you'll become more successful in the process. See Chapter 11 of this book for suggestions on how you can use our motivational products to say "Thank You" in a special way with very POSitive impact.

Another way to use the thank-you concept very effectively is to simply make it a point to write someone a thank-you note every day. Only 2% of the people in our population take time to write a thank-you note to somebody else for something they have done. By the way, when was the last time you sent someone a thank-you note? If you'll practice this one principle alone on a daily basis, you'll find that you'll feel better about yourself, others will respond to you more POSitively, and your success will be POSitively impacted.

Using someone's name, making comfortable eye contact, smiling at them, and saying thank you are simple ways we can build value with others. Become a trend setter in the world and practice these four ideas on a daily basis, and begin to share in the universal law that says, "When you give value to others, the value will be returned to you."

Yes, as I have said before, when you build POSitive attitudes toward yourself and others, success is semi-automatic.

> Find someone to help!
> Find an obstacle and a way to remove it!
> Look for a challenge and how to meet it!
> Find a problem and a way to solve it!
> Find a need and a way to fill it!
> It's a wonderful way to live.

Within that philosophy are the rich rewards of life. For to the degree you give other people what they need, they will give you what you need! This philosophy will continue to promote POSitive attitudes toward yourself, others and success.

IN REVIEW

Building POSitive attitudes towards success is a semi-automatic process and begins by building POSitive attitudes towards yourself and others. Let's review the three principles we just discussed in this chapter.

1. Develop your definite purpose. Purpose is the beginning of all success and must be as clear as possible. When you develop your purpose and strive towards its fulfillment on a daily basis, you automatically have more desire, become more enthusiastic and persistent in your quest for success. Remember that your purpose has emotional impact and is supported by your goals. It is a belief system that reflects what you value. Establish a minimum number of goals that are in line with your purpose so that each goal you accomplish brings you closer to fulfilling your purpose. Begin today to write out your purpose, and rewrite it and rewrite it until it becomes clear. In fact, why don't you start right now. My purpose is . . .

   _____

   _____

   _____

2. See failure as a stepping stone to success and not an obstacle. Review weekly how to connect all the dots in our exercise. If you can, it means that you are applying the principles we have discussed in this chapter. If you can't, go back and review the solution and think about how you are presently limiting yourself. Begin now by listing five ways you currently limit yourself.

   1. _____
   2. _____
   3. _____
   4. _____
   5. _____

3. Constantly put yourself in a serving role to others. It takes a big person to do this and the value received comes back in large amounts. Don't let your ego get in the way by feeling that others should give you something first. Put yourself in a leadership role by taking the first step toward serving others. Remember to use people's names, smile, use comfortable eye contact, and develop the habit of writing at least one thank-you note every day. A thank you note only takes three to four minutes of your time and a postage stamp.

In closing, remember to become aware of the many little successes you experience every day in your life. Concentrate on your own definition of success and don't become caught up in what others think success should be for you. Value your relationship with yourself and others, and I know you will begin to find success to be "semi-automatic!"

*If you can believe it and see it,
you can and will achieve it.*
                              Napoleon Hill

CHAPTER 5
USING CREATIVE VISUALIZATION
AND POSITIVE AFFIRMATIONS

(Anchors For Success)

    Upon the conclusion of the Vietnamese War, an Air Force captain who had been a prisoner of war for over seven years was being interviewed after a golf tournament by a national news reporter. The news reporter was being very skeptical of the captain's superb golf score as he had not played golf in over eight years. He was also very skeptical of a birdie the captain had made on the seventh hole. When the reporter said that he was surprised that he had shot so well, on the seventh hole, the captain replied, "I wasn't, because I have been playing (visualizing) that hole perfectly for the last seven years." The reporter's reply was, "I thought you said that you hadn't played golf in the last eight years?" The Air Force captain said, "Well, actually I haven't physically played the game in the last eight years, but I have been playing this hole (mentally) for the last seven years in my cell as a POW."

    Yes, it's true, this man as a POW had been visualizing his golf game for the last seven years right down to the very last detail. He saw himself positioned at each tee, he saw himself swing his club, and he pictured his ball gliding through the air to reach the destination that he wanted. As he visualized his game, he felt the swing of his club and he heard the crisp crack as his club made contact with the shiney white golf ball. He utilized all of his senses and brought them together in sharp focus through visualizing the successful outcome of his game, stroke by stroke.

    More and more successful people today use creative visualization and self affirmation principles to focus on their successes. Many Olympic athletes use these same principles to become medal winners in worldwide competition. Many business people use the same principles to focus on the outcomes they want in their business. As a sales person, I POSitively affirm the feelings I want created within my mental state and I visualize the outcomes I want to obtain. The majority of the time it works because I believe (belief system) creative visualization brings about the successes I desire.

Creative visualization is visualizing the outcome that you want to achieve step by step. For any event that you want to master, or any success that you want to achieve, simply visualize the steps you need to go through to obtain the successful outcome. It is necessary to visualize more than just the outcome. You must visualize with emotion every step of the outcome you want to achieve. For instance, as a speaker, I begin by visualizing in general the room I will be occupying during my presentation. I visualize the depth of the room, the make-up of the room, where people will be sitting, and how I will position myself in front of the group. I visualize the person introducing me and what I will see as I come up from the back of the room to the front to begin my program. I next visualize how the participants in my audience will be sitting and the expressions on their faces, concentrating on smiles and POSitive gestures. I visualize the exercises that we will be doing during my presentation and how the audience POSitively responds to them. As I conclude my presentation, I visualize people clapping and being enthusiastic about the program. I also associate my emotions with the outcome I want to achieve. I create the sound I want to hear from my audiences such as the applause, the laughter, and the sound of my voice as I speak to the audience. When you listen to your communication and visualize the outcome that you want to achieve, it makes a POSitive impression on your success mechanism (subconscious mind).

Using POSitive self-affirmations is also a part of preparing yourself for the successful outcome you want to achieve. POSitive self-affirmations are actually goals stated in the present tense. An example of this is a goal that a sales person may establish to make $100,000 per year. A POSitive affirmation of this goal would be said like this, "I am now making $100,000 per year." Stating what you want to achieve in the present tense is the self-affirmation. When it is repeated many times throughout the day every day, you begin to build a POSitive belief system which carries through into action. What we are doing is changing our thoughts to build a POSitive belief system which transfers to a POSitive attitude and gives us POSitive action and, therefore, becomes a POSitive anchor.

Simply write down whatever you want to achieve or accomplish *as if you were achieving it now* and repeat it to yourself 50 to 100 times a day. This requires self-discipline and a vein of POSitive thinking that you will achieve the outcome you are currently expressing to yourself.

Creative visualization and POSitive affirmations are what I consider basics. They are not new to us and you will find that many of these principles date back to the Bible. As you begin your new awareness in life, and your POSitive movement towards achieving those events that are important to you, you will find that these principles have a great deal of empowerment. When you practice them faithfully, you experience the results that are bound to come your way. *Remember, a clear image plus faith equals reality!*

IN REVIEW

1. Write up a POSitive affirmation you can repeat to yourself daily to bring about a postive outcome you desire.

   _____
   _____
   _____
   _____
   _____
   _____
   _____

2. Outline a successful event you want to achieve step by step. Now take each step and visualize it using mental pictures, sound and emotion. Practice this at night before you go to sleep and immediately upon waking in the morning. Practice this daily with conviction and watch what happens!

   STEPS
   1.

   2.

   3.

   4.

   5.

*If you have knowledge, let others
light their candles with it.*
                                Winston Churchill

CHAPTER 6
POSiTIVE MOTIVATIONAL SAYINGS

There are several things I do to build POSitive attitudes towards myself, others and success. One of the most beneficial vehicles I have found is to concentrate on motivational sayings that are simple yet have impact on my POSitive thinking towards life. I would like to take this opportunity to share these sayings with you.

Insist on yourself . . . never imitate . . .
Robert Anthony

~

Our only limitations are those which we set up in our minds
or permit others to establish for us.
Elizabeth Arden

~

The greatest thing on earth is a good idea.
St. Augustine

~

From visualization to realization is but a single step.
Al Schneider

Act the way you would like to be,
and soon you will be the way you act.
Author Unknown

~

The greatest mistake a person can make
is to be afraid of making one.
M. J. Babcock

~

Life is like the movies . . . we produce our own show . . .
Francis Bacon

~

Do not wait for the last judgement . . . it takes place every day.
Bruce Barton

~

Self-confidence in any enterprise comes, as a rule,
from remembrance of past success.
Baudjuin

~

Self-confidence is the first requisite to great undertakings.
Ludwig von Beethoven

~

Creative minds always have been able to survive
any kind of bad training.
St. Bernard

Change your mind and you change your life.
Christian N. Bovée

~

Be very choosey upon what you set your heart;
for if you want it strongly enough, you'll get it.
LaVerne Bowles

~

Thoughts are forces . . . they have form, quality, substance and power.
Jerry Brown

~

The happiest people are not the people without problems, but the
people who know how to solve their problems.
Leo Buscaglia

~

Inch by inch, anything is a cinch.
George Byron

~

To deny change is to deny the only single reality.
Albert Camus

~

If you have knowledge, let others light their candles with it.
Winston Churchill

~

We forfeit three-fourths of ourselves in order to be like other people.
Robert Cody

~

Find a need and fill it.
Dr. Joseph Collins

~

Planning a garden is like planning life. Arrange it to please yourself, copying not convention, tradition or any individual.
Malcolm Cowley

~

Everybody is one of a kind.
Dr. George Crane

~

The misfortunes hardest to bare are those which never come.
Richard Cumberland

~

What ever the mind can conceive and believe, the mind can achieve.
Dr. Napoleon Hill

~

Always think what you have to do is easy, and it will be so.
Rene Descartes

~

The buck stops here!
John Dewey

~

When engaging in any new adventure, discuss it only with those whose assistance is vital to its success.
Arthur Dobkin

~

Character is what you have when nobody is looking.
Marie Dresslar

~

The world belongs to the energetic.
Joni Eareckson

~

A great many people think they are thinking— when they are really rearranging their prejudice and superstitions.
Max Ehrmann

~

The victory of success is half won when one gains the habit of work.
George Eliot

~

Our purpose in life is not to get ahead of other people, but to get ahead of ourselves.
Nathaniel Emmons

~

The more we do, the more we can do.
Epictetus

~

If a man empties his purse into his head,
no man can take it away from him.
Dennis Fairchild

~

A wise man will make more opportunities than he finds.
Henry Ford

~

Chances are that right now you are standing
in the middle of your own acre of diamonds.
Harry Emerson Fosdick

~

What you can do or dream you can, begin it.
Boldness has genuis, power and magic in it.
Benjamin Franklin

~

According to your faith, be it unto you.
Buckminster Fuller

~

If we desire one thing and expect another,
we become like houses divided against ourselves.
Margaret Fuller

~

It is not a question of who is right, but what is right.
John Galbraith

~

Everything that has happened to you has come about because
you first saw it happening in your mind's eye.
Galileo

~

Habits are literally garments worn by our personalities . . .
we have them because they fit us.
Johann W. von Goeth

~

When the pupil is ready, the teacher appears.
Author Unknown

~

Success is a continuing upward spiral of progress.
Moritz Guedemann

~

Live your best, act your best and think your best today;
for today is the sure preparation for tomorrow.
Joseph Hall

Universal mind is operating through us
at the level of all our acceptance.
Nathaniel Hawthorne

~

We lie loudest when we lie to ourselves.
William Hazlitt

~

Yesterday is a cancelled check; tomorrow is a promissory note;
today is the only cash you have.
Eric Hoffer

~

They can conquer who believe they can.
J. G. Holland

~

When you copy another, you'll never find yourself.
Horace

~

No one is paid to sit around being capable of achievement.
Elbert Hubbard

~

Nothing in life is to be feared; only to be understood.
W. R. Inge

~

When you pray, move your feet.
Andrew Jackson

~

Life is not a problem to solve, but a mystery to experience.
William James

~

Nobody made you mad, you got mad!
Sir James Jeans

~

Worry is interest paid on trouble before it comes due.
Author Unknown

~

Every man in reality is two men. The man he is,
and the man he could be.
Eric Johnston

~

To be humble when you are praised is a great and rare achievement.
Carl Jung

~

A problem well stated is a problem half solved.
Henry J. Kaiser

~

The pessimist sees difficulty in every opportunity.
The optimist sees opportunity in every difficulty.
Charles Kettering

~

All things are possible to he who believes.
Jesus

~

To travel hopefully is better than to arrive.
Vince Lombardi

~

It takes energy to fail.
Samuel Lover

~

If you only care enough for the result,
you will most certainly achieve it.
Amy Lowell

~

Beaten paths are for beaten men.
Sir John Lubbock

~

There are not two, but three sides to every argument — yourself,
your opponent, somewhere in between — the truth.
Kay Lyons

There are two ways of meeting difficulties — you alter the difficulties,
or you alter yourself meeting them.
G. MacDonald

~

The things that haven't been done before are the things to try.
Dr. Maxwell Maltz

~

You can do nothing effectively without enthusiasm.
Mary Martin

~

I am master of my fate . . . I am the captain of my soul.
Giuseppi Mazzini

~

Originality is simply a pair of fresh eyes.
Margaret Mead

~

Demanding that greatness be turned loose within us
eventually releases something greater than we are.
H. L. Mencken

~

Life is but one continual course of instruction.
J. Stuart Mill

~

To be happy and successful develop the idea that every day
is going to be a great day.
Honore G. Mirabeau

~

It's not a question of how much a man knows,
but what use he makes of what he knows.
M. E. Montaigne

~

There can be no security where there is fear.
Edward R. Murrow

~

The use of money is all the advantage there is to having money.
Bill Moyers

~

People should think things out fresh, and not just accept conventional
terms in the conventional way of doing things.
Napoleon

~

Picture yourself vividly as winning, and that alone will contribute
immeasurably to success.
Friedrich Nietzsche

~

Your life is what your thoughts make of it.
Earl Nightingale

We first make our habits, and then our habits make us.
Charles Noble

~

We learn by doing things rather than by talking about them.
St. Paul

~

In life, as in chess — forethought wins.
Norman Vincent Peale

~

Always let your brain be captain, and never let your emotions mutiny against it.
Margaret Percival

~

Nothing is really work, unless you'd rather be doing something else.
Wilford Peterson

~

Small opportunities are often the beginnings of great enterprises.
William Lyons Phelps

~

What others say of me matters little.
What I say and do matters much.
Pittacus

~

Fear is the beginning of submission.
Catherine Ponder

~

Failure indicates that every energy has been poured
into the wrong channel.
Melvin Powers

~

Attitude isn't simply a state of mind, it is also a reflection
of what we value.
Rich Wilkins

~

We are what we repeatedly do. Excellence, then, is not an act,
but a habit.
W. B. Prescott

~

See it big, and keep it simple.
Proverbs

~

The formula for failure — try to please everybody.
Pasquier Quesnel

~

Being broke is a temporary situation, but poverty is a state of mind.
William J. Reilly

Free advice is usually worth what you paid for it.
Eleanor Roosevelt

~

Worry and hurry are twin task masters . . .
do not hire yourself out to them.
Franklin Roosevelt

~

I am bigger than anything that can happen to me.
Teddy Roosevelt

~

When you fight yourself, it's always a draw.
Leo Rosten

~

What I know doesn't impress me . . . what I don't know excites me.
Jean Jacques Rousseau

~

In every person is hidden a child who wants to play.
Dr. Harvey Ruben

~

Imagination is a form of faith.
Rosalind Russell

~

Bravery is being the only one who knows you are afraid.
J. C. von Schiller

~

He who is afraid to ask is ashamed of learning.
Sir Walter Scott

~

It's amazing how fast doors open to us
when we dare to take control of a situation.
David Seaburg

~

The answer is contained within the question.
Lucius A. Seneca

~

We may not see the kite, but we can feel the tug.
Dolly Sewell

~

Happiness is a state of mind in which our thinking is
pleasant a good share of the time.
William Shakespeare

~

If you want respect, have self-respect.
Richard B. Sheridan

~

Talent is what you possess — genius is what possesses you.
Harold Sherman

~

When you are through learning — you are through.
Dr. O. Carl Simonton

~

We are where we are and what we are
because of our habitual thinking.
Ralph Waldo Trine

~

The secret of success is consistency of purpose.
Thomas Troward

~

Human beings can alter their lives by altering their attitudes of mind.
Harry Truman

~

Associate yourself with people of good quality, for it is better to be
alone than in bad company.
Booker T. Washington

~

I think, therefore I am.
Rene Descartes

~

I must stand with anybody who stands right,
and part with him when he goes wrong.
Ella Wheeler Wilcox

~

Winning isn't everything, but wanting to win is.
Oscar Wilde

~

People are about as happy as they make up their minds to be.
Frank Lloyd Wright

~

Silence is often the greatest power.
Al Schneider

~

The talent of success is nothing more than doing what you do well,
and doing well whatever you do.
Harry Longfellow

~

Concentrating on successful experiences actually breeds
a strong sense of confidence.
Samuel T. Levin

~

The confidence we have in ourselves gives birth to much
of that we have in others.
F. LaRochefoucauld

Losing is a form of winning.
Al Schneider

~

The true genius does not look at his experiments as failures,
but as steppingstones to ultimate success.
Vera Dawson Tait

~

If you tell the truth, you don't have to remember anything.
Mark Twain

~

Our problem with change is not our inability, but our resistance.
Al Schneider

~

Our impulse to persuade others is strongest when
we have to persuade ourselves.
Eric Hoffer

~

Think in terms of poverty and you will live in poverty.
Napoleon Hill

~

To break a habit, create another one that will erase it.
Al Schneider

~

If you would create something, you must be something.
Johann Goethe

~

Make up your mind you can't — and you're always right.
Bob Goddard

~

Be sure to put your feet in the right place . . . And stand firm.
Abraham Lincoln

~

Listening is a lost skill which, in many people,
needs to be cultivated and nourished.
Lorraine Pfeiffer

~

An investment in knowledge always pays the best interest.
Benjamin Franklin

~

To be a person is to be engaged in a perpetual process of becoming.
Harry Emerson Fosdick

~

Life is a series of surprises.
Ralph Waldo Emerson

~

The only something you get for nothing is failure.
Arnold Glasgow

~

It is never too late to expand our horizons.
Author Unknown

~

To succeed — act as if it were impossible to fail.
Dorothea Brande

~

Reading is to the mind what exercise is to the body.
Sir Richard Steele

~

The surest way not to fail is to determine to succeed.
Richard B. Sheridan

~

There is nothing in the world more powerful than an idea whose time has come.
Red Motley

~

Do what you can with what you have, where you are.
Teddy Roosevelt

~

The actualizing of our potential can become the most exciting
adventure of our lifetime.
Herbert Otto

~

He who escapes a duty avoids a gain.
Theodore Parker

~

It's the set of the sails, not the swiftness of the gait,
which determines where we shall go.
Ruth Noordhoff

~

By the streets of "by and by" one arrives at the house of "never."
S. M. Cervantes

~

He who knows only his side of the case knows little of that.
J. Stuart Mill

~

Habit is the thing that makes us fear change,
regardless of the present condition of our lives.
William James

~

To change a habit, make a conscious decision,
then "act out" the new behavior.
Dr. Maxwell Maltz

There is only one success — to be able to spend your
life in your own way.
Christopher Morely

~

Things turn out best for the people who make
the best of the way things turn out.
John Wooden

~

Resentment is a cancer of the personality that is
as deadly as any physical growth.
Dr. James Stringham

~

Integrity is the first step to true greatness.
C. Simmons

~

You must have long-range goals to keep from being frustrated by
short-range failures.
Charles Noble

~

All we need to make us happy is something to be enthusiastic about.
Charles Kingsley

~

Home can be anywhere you make it.
Margaret Mead

When we reach out to life, life always reaches out to us.
Al Schneider

~

Every person stamps his value on himself.
J. C. Schiller

~

If your thought is saturated with fear of failure, it will neutralize your endeavors and make success impossible.
Baudjuin

~

The only thing we have to fear is fear itself.
Franklin Roosevelt

~

I have known a great many troubles — most of them never happened.
Mark Twain

~

Most of us are worrying about the future so much that we can't enjoy the present.
Harold Sherman

~

There is nothing permanent except change.
Will Rogers

~

Success doesn't consist in never making a mistake,
but in never making the same one a second time.
George Bernard Shaw

~

The only way one human being can properly attempt to influence
another is by encouraging him to think for himself.
Sir Leslie Stephen

~

Fear always springs from ignorance.
Ralph Waldo Emerson

~

By going over your day in imagination before you begin it,
you can begin acting successfully at any moment.
Dorothea Brande

~

Silence is the element in which great things fashion themselves.
Thomas Carlyle

~

Luck is when preparation and opportunity meet.
Earl Nightingale

~

Victory belongs to the most persevering.
Napoleon

I don't believe in circumstances.
George Bernard Shaw

~

When you make a mountain out of a mole hill, you have to climb it.
Sue Sikking

~

There is also a "second wind" of the mind.
Sheldon Shepard

~

Character building begins in infancy and continues until death.
Eleanor Roosevelt

~

Nothing is ever all wrong — even a stopped clock is right twice a day.
Author Unknown

~

No person will make a great business who wants to do it all himself or get all the credit.
Andrew Carnegie

~

Your profession is not who you are, it is only a costume.
Author Unknown

~

Hope is brightest when it dawns from fears.
Sir Walter Scott

~

Two aims in life: To get what you want, and to enjoy it.
Only the wisest achieve the second.
Logan P. Smith

~

Let us train our minds to desire what the situation demands.
Lucius Seneca

~

The fulfillment of your desire, the answer to your need,
has its conception in your imagination.
Charles Roth

~

Traditional Indian recipe for rabbit stew — first catch a rabbit . . .
Author Unknown

~

When angry, count to ten before you speak. If very angry,
count to one hundred.
Thomas Jefferson

~

When something (an affliction) happens to you, either let it defeat you,
or you defeat it. Even trivial things, if they express life, are good.
Rosalind Russell

The greatest punishment of laziness is witnessing the success of others who are less talented, but more industrious.
Sidney Harris

~

An idea is far more fertile if seduced rather than raped.
Edward DeBono

~

A winner never quits, and a quitter never wins.
Napoleon Hill

~

We cannot encourage another unless we have encouraged them in our own hearts.
Sarah Louise Arnold

~

When all is said and done, there is usually more said than done.
Author Unknown

~

There is no such thing as fear ... it is strong faith in catastrophe, real or imagined.
Al Schneider

~

Unbelief shuts the door to possibility.
Catherine Hubbell

We can do anything we want to if we stick to it long enough.
Helen Keller

~

Positive and negative are but two sides on the same coin — only facing different directions.
Willis Sloane

~

Whatever your lot in life — build on it.
Marvin Small

~

Friendship is higher than any other form of human love.
Socrates

~

You might not always get what you want, but you will always get what you expect.
Charles H. Spurgeon

~

Have the courage to live — anyone can die.
Harry H. Starret

~

Attitude determines your altitude.
Sir Richard Steele

~

Courage is the fondest of human qualities because it
guarantees all of the others.
Sir Leslie Stephen

~

If you are a self made person, a larger self has made you.
Robert L. Stevenson

~

It doesn't matter what happens to you — it only matters
what happens through you.
Harriet Beecher Stowe

~

Obstacles are those terrifying things we see when we take
our eyes off of our goal.
Dr. James A. Stringham

~

My estimate of the human race is a duplicate
of my estimate of myself.
Ben Sweetland

~

If you love your work, vacations are an intrusion.
Herbert Swope

~

The thing to do is to supply light and not heat.
Vera Dawson Tait

Nothing succeeds so well as success.
Talleyrand-Périgord

~

You have to experience some lows,
in order to appreciate your highs.
Author Unknown

~

The mind attracts to one the exact material equivalent
to that which one thinks about most often.
Author Unknown

~

Suggestion works always in terms of what is dominant
in a person's consciousness.
Author Unknown

~

When we are truly involved in change, it is a wonderful
and satisfying experience.
Author Unknown

~

Demonstrate where you are, because you are there,
whether you realize it or not.
Author Unknown

~

Never flee from something — flee to something.
Author Unknown

~

With the time and energy we spend in making failure a certainty, we might have certain success.
Author Unknown

~

Every negative emotion stems from fear.
William James

~

Anyone who keeps on learning remains young, regardless of age.
Author Unknown

~

No legacy is as rich as honesty.
Author Unknown

~

After receiving recognition, you may not be a different person, but others will perceive you as if you are.
Author Unknown

~

Truth is generally the best vindication against slander.
Author Unknown

~

I discovered that the more I hustled, the luckier I seemed to get.
Fran Tarkenton

~

Having a clear mental image of a goal is an indispensable step toward achieving it.
Napoleon Hill

~

Difficulties and responsibilities strengthen and enrich the mind.
Dr. Norman Vincent Peale

~

People who never do anything more than they are paid to do, are never paid for anything more than they do.
Author Unknown

~

With all things, it is better to hope than to despair.
Author Unknown

~

It's not what happens to us that counts, it's our reaction to it.
Author Unknown

~

It's not how much we have, but how much we enjoy that makes happiness.
Author Unknown

Change your thoughts and you change your world.
William James

~

If you are going to succeed, you have got to first
feel good about yourself.
Author Unknown

~

The present moment is all we have . . . the past and future have
meaning because they are part of the present.
Author Unknown

~

Hold a picture of yourself long and steadily enough in your mind's
eye, and you will be drawn toward it.
Napoleon Hill

~

There is nothing more vulnerable than entrenched success.
Author Unknown

~

That man/woman is truly free who desires what he/she is able to
perform, and does what he/she desires.
Author Unknown

~

In releasing old ways, and letting go of the past, we do not lose the good we have gained.
Author Unknown

~

Creativeness often consists of merely turning up what is already there.
Author Unknown

~

Preparation for something better begins with gratitude for what we have.
Author Unknown

~

More than anything else in life, it is the habit of worry that keeps us from being happy.
Author Unknown

~

Deep within us is the seed of greatness.
Rich Wilkins

~

Whenever you possess conviction and belief about something, you will experience it.
Author Unknown

~

A person can succeed at most anything for which they have unlimited enthusiasm.
Dr. Norman Vincent Peale

To understand an individual human being,
lay aside all scientific knowledge of the average man.
Author Unknown

~

It is easier to write your principles down, than to live up to them.
Author Unknown

~

Name it and claim it . . .
Elaine Hibbard

~

Your future is only as bright as your mind is open.
Rich Wilkins

~

To love oneself is the beginning of a lifelong romance.
Oscar Wilde

~

Thinking is an experiment dealing with small quantities of energy,
just as a general moves miniature figures over a map before
setting his troops in action.
Sigmund Freud

~

Every good thought you think is contributing its share to the
ultimate result of your life.
Greenville Kleiser

The mind is its own place, and in itself can make heaven of Hell,
and a hell of Heaven.
Milton

~

Most of the time we think we're sick, it's all in the mind.
Thomas Wolfe

~

To hate and to fear is to be psychologically ill. It is, in fact,
the consuming illness of our time.
H. A. Overstreet

~

Habit with him was all the test of truth,
"It must be right: I've done it from my youth."
George Crabbe

~

To fall into a habit is to begin to cease to be.
Miguel de Unamuno

~

Most people live, whether physically, intellectually or morally, in a very restricted circle of their potential being. They make use of a very small portion of their possible consciousness, and of their soul's resources in general, much like a man who, out of his world bodily organism, should get into the habit of using and moving only his little finger. Great emergencies and crises show us how much greater our vital resources are than we had supposed.
William James

Enlighten the people generally, and tyranny and oppressions of body and mind will vanish like evil spirits at the dawn of the day.
Thomas Jefferson

~

Great men are they who see that spiritual is stronger than any material force, that thoughts rule the world.
Emerson

~

All that is comes from the mind; it is based on the mind, it is fashioned by the mind.
The Pali Canon

~

Follow your desires as long as you live; do not lessen the time of following desires, for the wasting time is an abomination to the spirit.
Ptahhotpe

~

It is common sense to take a method and try it. If it fails, admit it frankly and try another. But above all, try something.
Franklin D. Roosevelt

~

Bring me my bow of burning gold, bring me my arrows of desire, bring me my spear — O clouds, unfold! Bring me my chariot of fire!
William Blake

~

Of all escape mechanisms, death is the most efficient.
H. L. Mencken

~

The strangest and most fantastic fact about negative emotions is that people actually worship them.
P. D. Ouspensky

~

You have no idea what a poor opinion I have of myself — and how little I deserve it.
W. S. Gilbert

~

The childhood shows the man, as morning shows the day.
John Milton

~

There is perhaps nothing so bad and so dangerous in life as fear.
Jawaharlal Nehru

~

There is no cure for birth and death save to enjoy the interval.
George Santayana

~

The music that can deepest reach, and cure all ill, is cordial speech.
Emerson

~

Healing is a matter of time, but it is sometimes also
a matter of opportunity.
Hippocrates

~

Fear is the main source of superstition, and one of the main sources
of cruelty. To conquer fear is the beginning of wisdom.
Bertrand Russell

~

Yea, though I walk through the valley of the shadow of death,
I will fear no evil: for thou art with me;
thy rod and thy staff they comfort me.
Psalm 23

~

Death and taxes and childbirth!
There's never any convenient time for any of them.
Scarlett O'Hara

~

One should sympathize with the joy, the beauty, the color of life —
the less said about life's sores the better.
Oscar Wilde

~

Try thinking of love or something
Christopher Fry

~

What a wonderful life I've had! I only wish I'd realized it sooner.
Colette

~

Optimism, said Candide, is a mania for maintaining that all is well when things are going badly.
Voltaire

~

An optimist may see a light where there is none, but why must the pessimist always run to blow it out?
Michel De Saint-Pierre

~

We are healed of a suffering only by experiencing it to the full.
Marcel Proust

~

Destiny is not a matter of chance, it is a matter of choice; it is not a thing to be waited for, it is a thing to be achieved.
William Jennings Bryan

~

Death is not the greatest loss in life. The greatest loss is what dies inside us while we live.
Norman Cousins

~

He who has a why to live can bear almost any how.
Nietzsche

Love thy neighbor as thyself, but choose your neighborhood.
Louise Beal

~

I only have "yes" men around me. Who needs "no" men?
Mae West

~

I don't like work — no man does — but I like what is in work, the chance to find yourself. Your own reality — for yourself, not for others — what no other man can ever know.
Joseph Conrad

~

I will work in my own way, according to the light that is in me.
Lydia Maria Child

~

The spirit of self-help is the root of all genuine growth in the individual; and, exhibited in the lives of many, it constitutes the true source of national vigor and strength. Help from without is often enfeebling in its effects, but help from within invariably invigorates.
Samuel Smiles

~

I am different from Washington; I have a higher, grander standard of principle. Washington could not lie. I can lie, but I won't.
Mark Twain

~

We can secure other people's approval, if we do right and try hard; but our own is worth a hundred of it.
Mark Twain

~

Love truth, but pardon error.
Voltaire

~

Do what you can, with what you have, with where you are.
Theodore Roosevelt

~

God, give us grace to accept with serenity the things that cannot be changed, courage to change the things which should be changed, and the widsom to distinguish the one from the other.
Reinhold Niebuhr

~

Harmony is pure love, for love is complete agreement.
Lope de Vega

~

The greatest pleasure I know is to do a good action by stealth, and to have it found out by accident.
Charles Lamb

~

I always say, keep a diary and someday it'll keep you.
Mae West

~

There are some days when I think I'm going to die from an overdoes of satisfaction.
Salvadore Dali

~

I cannot give you the formula for success, but I can give you the formula for failure — which is: Try to please everybody.
Herbert Bayard Swope

~

One must not lose desires. They are mighty stimulants to creativeness, to love and to long life.
Alexander Bogomoletz

~

Nothing contributes so much to tranquilize the mind as a steady purpose — a point on which the soul may fix its intellectual eye.
Mary Wollstonecraft Shelley

~

The secret of success is constancy to purpose.
Benjamin Disraeli

~

We must cultivate our garden.
Voltaire

When you get right down to the root of the meaning of the word "succeed," you find it simply means to follow through.
F. W. Nichol

~

Even if you're on the right track,
you'll get run over if you just sit there.
Will Rogers

~

The destiny of mankind is not decided by material computation. We learn that we are spirits, not animals, and that something is going on in space and time, and beyond space and time, which, whether we like it or not, spells duty.
Winston Churchill

~

There is no failure except in no longer trying.
Elbert Hubbard

~

I believe that anyone can conquer fear by doing the things he fears to do, provided he keeps doing them until he gets a record of successful experiences behind him.
Eleanor Roosevelt

~

Faith is an excitement and an enthusiasm: it is a condition of intellectual magnificence to which we must cling as to a treasure, and not squander in the small coin of empty words.
George Sand

As the body without the spirit is dead,
so faith without works is dead also.
James 2:26

~

He that lives upon hope will die fasting.
Benjamin Franklin

~

Hope is a good breakfast, but it is a bad supper.
Francis Bacon

~

Do all of the good you can, by all the means you can, in all the ways you can, in all the places you can, at all times you can, to all the people you can, as long as ever you can.
John Wesley

~

Lord, make me an instrument of Your peace.
Where there is hatred let me sow love;
where there is injury, pardon;
where there is doubt, faith;
where there is despair, hope;
where there is darkness, light;
and where there is sadness, joy.
St. Francis of Assisi

~

Do not take life too seriously. You will never get out of it alive.
Elbert Hubbard

So long as we love we serve; so long as we are loved by others,
I would almost say that we are indispensable;
and no man is useless while he has a friend.
Robert Louis Stevenson

~

Independence? That's middle-class blasphemy. We are all
dependent on one another, every soul of us on earth.
George Bernard Shaw

~

The growth of the human mind is still high adventure,
in many ways the highest adventure on earth.
Norman Cousins

~

No man is a failure who is enjoying life.
William Feather

~

If I had to define life in a word, it would be: Life is creation
Claude Bernard

~

A noble person attracts noble people,
and knows how to hold on to them.
Goethe

~

The mind of man is capable of anything —
because everything is in it, all the past as well as the future.
Joseph Conrad

~

A faithful friend is the medicine of life.
Ecclesiastes 6:16

~

There is nothing so powerful as truth — and often nothing so strange.
Daniel Webster

~

If at first you don't succeed your running about average.
M. H. Alderson

~

Personally, I'm always ready to learn,
although I do not always like being taught.
Winston Churchill

~

The control man has secured over nature has
far out run his control over himself.
Ernest Jones

~

Life is like playing a violin in public and
learning the instrument as one goes on.
Samuel Butler

People don't like to be sold, however, they sure love to buy.
Rich Wilkins

Our purpose in life is not to get ahead of other people — but to get ahead of ourselves.
Nathaniel Emmons

CHAPTER 7
GIVING MORE ENERGY TO COMPANY MEETINGS

SUGGESTION #1

Attitude is an end result

EXERCISE OBJECTIVE: To help people understand that your attitude is a function of your thinking. You can introduce the following model in your meeting on a flip chart or overhead projector.

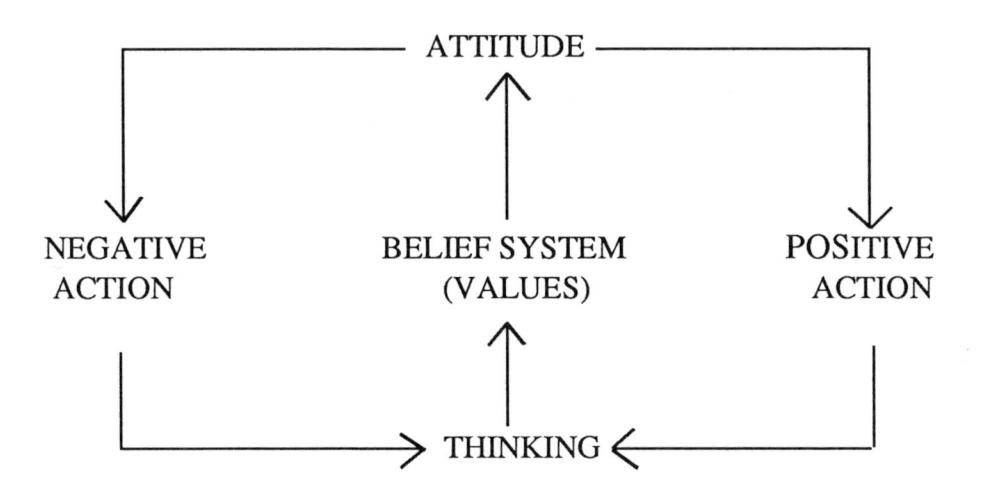

```
            ┌──────── ATTITUDE ────────┐
            │            ↑             │
            ↓            │             ↓
        NEGATIVE    BELIEF SYSTEM    POSITIVE
         ACTION       (VALUES)        ACTION
            │            ↑             │
            └──────→  THINKING ←───────┘
```

William James, the founder of modern psychology, said, "You can change people's attitudes only by changing their thinking." He is absolutely right, and the way that an attitude is formed is through thoughts that are repeated several times which begin to be noticed by others as our attitudes. As this process is repeated with the same thinking, we develop a belief system which becomes a reflection of what we value.

There are many examples of what we are saying. If you keep telling yourself that you will not make $50,000 a year, or that you'll never get that sales job, or that you'll never get the promotion because you don't feel that you are worthy of a promotion, this becomes a belief system which begins with your thinking and is transformed into the result (your attitude) that you keep thinking about. The way to change our attitudes about everything is to change our thinking about the outcome that we want to achieve. It's a very simple model and has high impact when people understand it.

This is a good example to raise your group's awareness level of how our attitudes develop. Keep in mind that the first time you do this not everyone will agree because we are conditioned to think that things like this are complex and they have been set in place since the beginning of time. It's true they have been around since the beginning of time, but everything is only as complex as we make it. Our attitudes may be complex, but how we form them is not. You might want to take examples within your own company environment of past experiences of things that your company has achieved or has not achieved and take it through the above model.

SUGGESTION #2

Attitude does make the difference!

EXERCISE OBJECTIVE: To help people understand that our attitude is the foundation of all success and failure.

This is a fun exercise and can be used to kick off a meeting with a lot of energy and get your audience very involved in understanding that our attitudes are the foundation of all success. For this exercise you will need a flip chart to write on or an overhead projector if you have a larger group.

Write on the top of your flip chart (overhead): "Here is what makes the difference!" Tell them that this is a participative exercise in which you need their help in designing a very successful person in life. Ask them to picture in their mind (emotional impact) the person that they have a great deal of respect for because they are highly successful. Ask them to think about a one-word characteristic that makes this person highly successful. By the way, stop and ask the group how many people immediately thought of themselves as successful when you asked them to picture in their mind a successful person. I'll bet only about 2% of your audience thought about themselves, because most people do not see themselves as successful. Now, ask them to begin sharing these characteristics with you. As they begin giving you the characteristics, write them down on the flip chart. You may hear words like *enthusiastic, empathetic, honest, humorous, caring, driven, assertive*, etc. Get them to list as many characteristics as possible. In my experience most groups will come up with two to three pages of characteristics.

When the group slows down or they come to an end, tell them that you need additional help from them. Tell them that you want to go back through the list of characteristics to determine individually if these characteristics are a reflection of their attitudes or their skills. Step up to the flip chart, start with the first characteristic and say, "Is this an attitude or a skill?" Once they decide, go to the second and so forth. You will find that 80% to 90% of the characteristics are a result of *attitudes* that these successful people have.

The important point to remember is to finalize the exercise by reminding them that the characteristics successful people develop are the result of their attitudes. Attitudes are the foundation of all of our successes and failures in life. The terrific thing is that our attitude is a skill. That's right! Our attitude is a skill that needs to be developed and reinforced every day. Just as people go to the gym to work out physically daily, we as successful people need to go the mental gym to work out mentally every day.

To help stimulate the audience, I use what I call my VALUE PACK. It is a pad of fifty brand new, crisp one dollar bills glued along the edges and put inside of a plastic folder with a cover that says "Golden Value

Pack." As people begin to give me characteristics such as *empathy, honesty, caring*, or other characteristics which are "values related," I make a big deal of pulling my value pack out of my pocket, slowly tearing a dollar bill off of the pad and putting it into their hand. This gets people excited about giving you more characteristics and raises energy levels tremendously in the room. Should you be interested in purchasing a value pack from us, simply call our office (502-955-7269) and we will give you additional details. This is a great way to motivate any audience.

SUGGESTION #3

Who is your biggest competitor?

EXERCISE OBJECTIVE: To help people understand that they are their biggest competitor.

This exercise is the result of talking with thousands of people around the country about their competition. Most people think that other people and companies are their biggest competitors. This exercise helps them understand that we are our own biggest competitor because we limit ourselves more than anyone else does.

This exercise was also included in Chapter 3, "Developing POSitive Attitudes Toward Success." It was in the second principle entitled, "Seeing Failure as a Stepping Stone to Success Instead of an Obstacle." This exercise requires a flip chart, or overhead projector if you have a larger group. You can begin the session or conversation by asking them, "Who is your biggest competitor?" Should they give you other people and companies, write them down on the flip chart. However, within a short period of time usually someone in the audience says, "Well, I am my biggest competitor." Should you have one of our value packs, please appreciate this person with a $1 bill. This will stimulate more creative thinking in the group as your presentation progresses.

Explain to your audience that it is a perception that other people and other companies are our competitors. However, we must understand that our biggest competitor is ourselves. Ask them why. Confirm and reaffirm their reasons and sum it up by reminding them that we beat ourselves up mentally, and we put ourselves down more than anyone else. This is a conditioned response left over from our childhood years and quite frankly, we are conditioned to think "no" before we think "yes" when presented with a challenge. You can prove this to them by simply asking them this powerful question. "By the time you were five years old, how many times did you hear the word NO?" You'll get answers such as, thousands of times, hundreds of thousands of times, and millions of times. They are all absolutely right! You see, we are conditioned to the word NO which negatively impacts our attitudes, and our initial belief systems. At this point, move over to your flip chart or overhead and tell them that you are going to graphically show them that they are their greatest competitor because they impose their own limitations on themselves. Explain that to be more successful in life, they must go beyond their self-imposed limitations to achieve more successful events in life.

Put the following nine dots on your flip chart or overhead.

•   •   •

•   •   •

•   •   •

Challenge your audience to connect all of the dots with four straight lines without taking their pen off the paper. Repeat it to them again, and tell them that you just gave them the solution to this opportunity by reminding them that they are their biggest competitor. Even if some people in your audience have seen this opportunity in the past, very few of them remember the solution because it is so simple. After about 15 seconds, help them with the solution to this opportunity, as we don't want to intimidate members of the audience. Ask them what "figure" they see when they look at these nine dots. You will hear people say, "a box or a square." Relate to them that as soon as they saw the nine dots as a box or a square, they have automatically defeated themselves because boxes and squares have sides that limit people. The solution to this opportunity is to go beyond the sides (our self imposed limitations) like this.

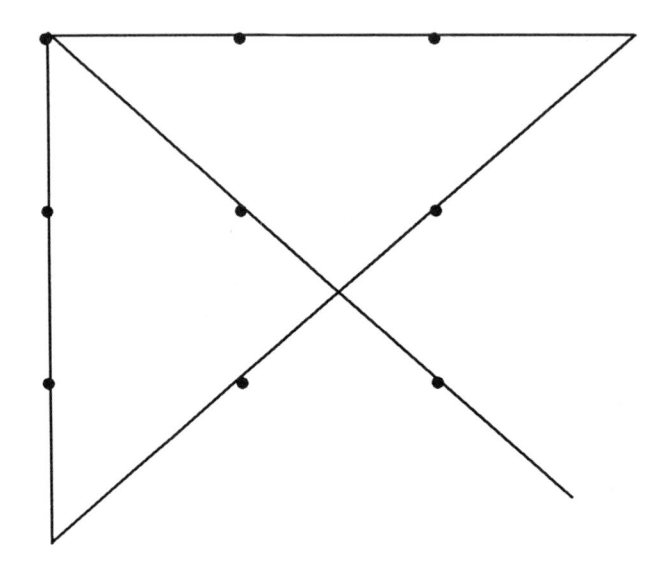

Now, explain to them that the solution to this challenge was not the main point that you wanted to deliver. The main point is that the box also is an example of our comfort zone as I have indicated below.

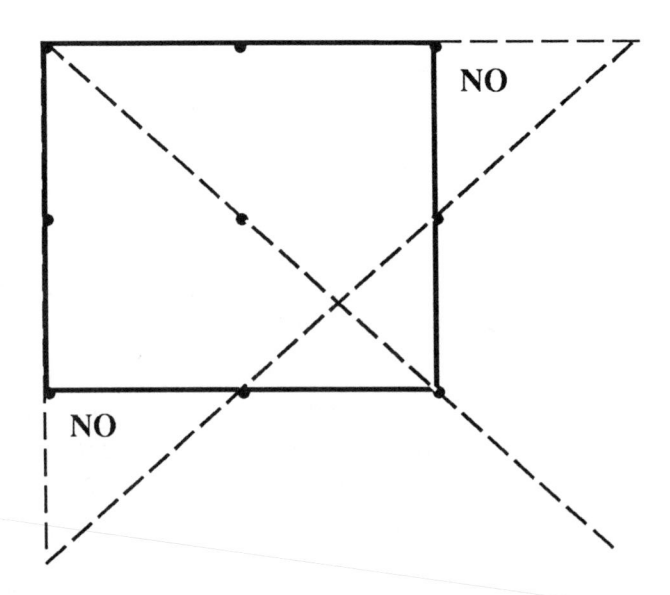

Ask your audience to give you examples of some comfort zones that they have witnessed. You will probably hear things like *friends, our homes, our offices, our daily routine, driving to work the same way every day, eating at the same restaurant most of the time,* and more importantly, *the people that we hang around with routinely on a daily basis.* Help your audience understand that successful people move out of their comfort zone on a daily basis to stretch themselves and grow. Encourage them to move into the two triangular areas outside of the box in the above diagram which is what I call our "no" zones. These are the two areas that are going to cause you to stretch and grow, and you will constantly hear the word NO from others. You can sum up this exercise by relating to them that all successful people have heard the word "no" hundreds of thousands of times. Examples of these people are Thomas Edison, Henry Ford, the Wright Brothers, Walt Disney, Lee Iacocca, and Col. Harland Sanders. Harland Sanders heard the word "no" over a thousand times before he got his first "yes" from a small restaurant that said they would pay him a nickel per chicken for his herbs and spices recipe, and look what happened in his great adventure!

SUGGESTION #4

We live in a straight line world

EXERCISE OBJECTIVE: To get your audience to understand that we live in a world filled with conditioned thinking.

Several years ago my daughter and I got into a discussion about how we condition ourselves to think a certain way. Often we are presented with a problem that requires unusual thinking. Because we get conditioned to see things a certain way the majority of the time, we find it difficult to find the solution to a problem when it requires a different approach or a different angle for its solution.

The following is a great example of perceived communication that really hinders our creative process when looking for solutions to our problems. My daughter brought this home from school one day and I couldn't come up with a solution because I am an adult who is conditioned to think a certain way. She said, "Dad, this is the roman numeral nine (IX); can you change it into a six with one line?" I looked at this roman numeral nine for several minutes and I couldn't figure it out. My daughter took the pen from my hand and she said, "Dad, it's simple, all you have to do is this (SIX)."

The above example demonstrates that we have a tendency to make things very complex. Because we see straight lines, we think the solution should be in terms of straight lines. However, as we can see, it requires a curved line. We need to open up our minds when we hear people making straight line statements to us such as,

> "You're not smart enough to go to college."
> "If you are so smart, how come your aren't rich."
> "We've tried it that way and it doesn't work."
> "Your price is too high."
> "You are too short to play basketball."

All of the above are straight line statements that require the very simple solution of curved line thinking. When people in your work environment seem to be hung up on traditional ways of doing things, simply use this example to help them understand that sometimes we have to break the rules to come up with the solutions that are mutually beneficial.

The above four suggestions are tremendously effective when used in your company meetings to help people understand how to build POSitive attitudes towards themselves, others and success. I suggest that you think these suggestions through, practice them before you use them with people, and position them with a personal story or example of what you've seen in your lifetime. Don't worry, you've got plenty of personal stories you can use. Think about the tremendous experiences you've had in life to bring about your own successes and failures.

I also encourage you to use these examples repeatedly at sales, marketing and operations meetings. You will be surprised at how few people remember the solutions to the challenges you have presented to them. A way to "anchor" the principles with your group is to use our attitude pins, plaques and posters found in Chapter 11 as daily reminders of what you have shared with them.

Chances are that right now you are standing in the middle of your own acres of diamonds.
Dr. Alex Cromwell

CHAPTER 8
HOW TO USE OUR GOLDEN ATTITUDE LAPEL PINS℠ FOR MAXIMUM IMPACT

Our GOLDEN ATTITUDE LAPEL PIN℠ is currently being worn by more than 100,000 people worldwide to build POSitive attitudes towards themselves, others and success. Here are over 30 ways our clients have told us they use our attitude pin to impact people in their personal and professional lives:

* Make a spontaneous gift of a pin (take the one off your own lapel or blouse) and give it to a good customer.

* Give a pin to the secretaries and/or receptionists in your prospects' offices who are especially helpful.

* Present pins to key co-workers in your office who make the sales process run smoothly (shipping, personnel, receptionists, secretaries, etc.).

* Award a pin to vendors or suppliers who assist your sales with timely service.

* Pin one on the sun visor of your car (or other conspicuous place), near your desk, in your daily calendar book or anywhere you are sure to look every day.

* Make a gift of a pin to customers' secretaries who are especially helpful.

* Give pins to an associate or peer who needs a boost.

* Enclose a pin to a prospect along with your proposal for new business.

* Award a pin to any member of a civic, social or charitable organization you belong to who shows exceptional service or dedication.

* Present a pin to a local athlete or student for an exceptional performance.

* Award one to the supervisor who handles a tough problem especially well.

* Give one to the employee who helps save a good customer's business (or brings one back!).

* Make a gift of one to the secretary who's always doing good deeds.

* Present one to the customer who regularly stimulates referrals for you.

* Give one to the service team member who solves that stubborn problem.

* Award one to the employee who reminds everyone that quality

control is everyone's job.

* Give one to the vendor who appreciates your business by sending you some referrals.

* Award one to each member of the sales or service team that breaks a performance goal.

* Give one to the technician who returns from school and readily shares his/her new knowledge

* Make sure the person with the biggest smile in the office always has on a pin.

* Give one to any employee that scores high on their evaluation.

* Wear one yourself!

* Put one in your top salesperson's pay envelope.

* Make them part of your personnel evaluation process.

* Award one for the "most improved attitude" among your sales staff.

* Give one to each new sales person as part of their orientation.

* Present one to your top clerical person or best sales receptionist.

* Make a spontaneous gift of a pin for an exceptional effort or achievement.

* Award one to the weekly sales leader.

* Present one for the completion of additional training or schooling.

* Give one to key vendors and suppliers who give exceptional service.

BONUS: Each time you present a GOLDEN ATTITUDE LAPEL PIN℠ to an employee, give an EXTRA PIN with instructions to present the pin to someone who exhibits a Golden Attitude.

We receive letters and phone calls from people daily telling us how their attitude pin has impacted their lives. Should you not be familiar with our GOLDEN ATTITUDE LAPEL PIN℠ and you want additional information, or to place an order, refer to page 146 or, please call our office at (502)955-7269 or FAX us at (502)955-9795

ATTITUDE
by
Rich Wilkins

ATTITUDE isn't simply a state of mind . . . it is also a reflection of what we value. Attitude is more than just saying I can, it is believing you can. It requires believing before seeing, because seeing is based on circumstances, believing is based on faith. Attitude is so contagious especially when we allow it to turn our doubts of the past into passions of today and set the stage for our tomorrows. We have total ownership of our attitudes. No one else has the power to alter our attitudes without our permission. Our attitude allows us to become more empowering than money, to rise above our failures, and accept others for who they are, and what they say. It is more important than giftedness and is the forerunner of all skills needed for happiness and success. Our attitudes can be used to build us up or put us down - the choice is ours. It also gives us the wisdom to know that we can't change events of the past. I am convinced that life is 10% what happens to me, and 90% how I respond to it . . . and it is with this state of mind that I remain in charge of my ATTITUDES.

(PLAQUE #1)

Actual Sizes:
Plaques 9" x 12"
Posters 8½" x 11"

A GOLDEN ATTITUDE IS...

Always making today your best day
Taking pride in a job well done
Treating others with respect
Isolating your negative thoughts
Treating every new task as an opportunity
Utilizing your talents daily
Doing the job right the first time
Expecting positive outcomes daily
Speaking well of others everyday

(PLAQUE #2)

CHAPTER 9
FIFTEEN WAYS TO USE OUR POSTERS AND PLAQUES TO POSITIVELY IMPACT OTHERS AROUND YOU

Ideas are the beginning of everything. I once heard Earl Nightingale say that people pluck ideas out of a conversation like an expert fisherman snags fish out of a fast moving stream. As we learn new ideas and practice principles, they are more easily retained by using an "anchoring" device to remind us of their importance. We have designed a line of posters and plaques which can be used to anchor our nine step definition of a GOLDEN ATTITUDE and to further understand that *your attitude isn't simply a state of mind, it is also a reflection of what you value.* You will find examples of what our plaques and posters say on page 136, with ideas on how to use them on the next page.

The following are several ways you can use our posters and plaques to POSitively impact yourself and others around you.

- Place them in company breakrooms

- Place them by the time clock as POSitive reminders

- Place them in conference rooms for others to see

- Place them in training rooms to POSitively reinforce your training process

- Place them in customer service areas as reminders of how important your customers are

- Place them in the reception area of your company so that people who visit witness the innovation of your company

- Place them in your home and children's room as a constant reminder of how important POSitive thinking is to your family.

- Send one to a business associate to thank them for doing business with you

- Send one to a hard to see prospect to get their attention and to let them know that you have a great attitude towards them

- Send one to a friend who may be feeling down or is going through a very difficult time

- Give one to a company team member who has gone the extra mile in their job

- Use it to recognize "the employee of the month" in your company

- Use it to recognize the person who has just received a promotion to reinforce the POSitive attitudes they are going to bring to their new position

- Use it to hang in your own office to POSitively reinforce yourself

- Send one to a vendor who has given you exceptional service

*If a man empties his purse into his head,
no man can take it away from him.*
Benjamin Franklin

CHAPTER 10
PERSONAL AND PROFESSIONAL DEVELOPMENT RESOURCES

Suggested Books

I Dare You by William Danforth
A Kick in The Seat of The Pants by Roger Von Oech
The One Minute Manager by Kenneth Balanchard
Playing to Win by Fran Tarkenton
How To Win Friends And Influence People by Dale Carnegie
Dress For Success by John P. Molloy
The Magic of Getting What You Want by David Schwartz
Psycho-Cybernetics by Dr. Maxwell Maltz
Smart Moves by Dr. Lyle Sussman
Dare to Discipline by Dr. James Dobson
The Language of Feelings by Dr. David Viscott
Signals by Allen Pease
Managing by Harold Geneen
Confessions of a Happy Christian by Zig Ziglar
The Greatest Salesman in the World by Og Mandino
Positive Imaging by Norman Vincent Peale
How To Get Control of Your Time and Your Life by Allen Lakein
Top Performance by Zig Ziglar
See You At The Top by Zig Ziglar
Raising Positive Kids In A Negative World by Zig Ziglar
The Inspirational Writings of Robert Schuller by Robert Schuller
Earl Nightingale's Greatest Discovery by Earl Nightingale

A Kid's Goal-Setting Guide by Lanson Ross
Think and Grow Rich by Dr. Napoleon Hill
The Power of Your Subconscious Mind by Dr. Joseph Murphy
Strategic Selling by Robert B. Miller
How I Raised Myself from Failure to Success in Selling by Frank Bettger
When Smart People Fail by Carole Hyatt
How to Develop Self-Confidence and Influence People by Public Speaking by Dale Carnegie
The Best Seller by Ron Willingham
The Psychology of Winning by Dr. Dennis Waitley
You Can't Afford the Luxury of a Negative Thought by Peter McWilliams
Nonmanipulative Selling by Tony Alessandra
Creative Visualization by Shakti Gawein
Personal Selling Power 1-800-752-7355 (Published eight times per year.)

Audio Cassette Tape Programs

All the following programs can be ordered from Nightingale Conant Corporation, 7300 N. Lehigh Avenue, Chicago, Illinois 60648, 800-572-2770.

"Mission Success" by Og Mandino
"The Power of Desire" by Jack Zufelt
"The Power of Optimism" by Allen McGinnis
"How To Be A No Limit Person" by Dr. Wayne Dyer
"The Psychology of Winning" by Dr. Dennis Waitley
"The Strangest Secret" by Earl Nightingale
"How To Master Your Time" by Brian Tracy
"The Psychology of Success" by Brian Tracy
"How To Raise Happy, Healthy, Self-Confident Children" by Brian Tracy
"Unlimited Power" by Anthony Robbins
"The Winning Attitude" by Art Mortell
"See You At The Top" by Zig Ziglar
"The Psychology of Selling" by Brian Tracy
"Nonmanipulative Selling" by Tony Alessandra

When the student is ready the teacher appears.
　　　　　　　　　　　　　Author Unknown

CHAPTER 11
MOTIVATIONAL PRODUCTS

THE "CLASSIC" GOLDEN ATTITUDE LAPEL PIN

Why do some people make POSitive things happen and others never get started? It's because of their ATTITUDE... and that is just what our attitude pin can do for you and the members of your company. Currently over 150,000 people worldwide are wearing our GOLDEN ATTITUDE LAPEL PIN on a daily basis to POSitively impact themselves, others and success. For only $5.00, we will guarantee your GOLDEN ATTITUDE for life. That's right! Should you lose your GOLDEN ATTITUDE LAPEL PIN or break it, we will replace it free. Also, use our attitude pin in your company to...

- Add POSitive impact to company meetings
- Empower company attittudes and morale
- Create POSitive staying power
- Create higher energy levels

Volume discounts are as follows:

1 - 100 Pins $5.00
100 - 299 Pins $4.75
300 - 499 Pins $4.50
500 Plus Pins $4.00

THE PLASTIC GOLDEN ATTITUDE PIN

ATTITUDE℠
By Rich Wilkins & Company

    The plastic ATTITUDE pin is the result of our customers' requests for an attitude pin that could be used in large corporations, government agencies and school systems. It is priced very reasonably which allows it to be purchased in larger quantities on a more cost effective basis. If you want to have a POSitive impact on large numbers of people in your organization, this product will give you an excellent return on your investment. The plastic ATTITUDE pin makes a nice reinforcement tool especially when you bring in "MR POS" to kick off your attitude building program in your company. For more information on our attitude building programs see page 153.
    Volume discounts are as follows:

    Minimum — 100 Pins $2.00 Ea.
    250 + Pins $1.75
    500 + Pins $1.50
    1000 + Pins $1.00

    Each attitude pin comes attached to a card with our 9 step definition of a GOLDEN ATTITUDE!

MOTIVATIONAL VIDEO #1

Give your next company meeting a POSitive impact with "MR POS"! In his new video, "MR POS" brings you SIX powerful motivational messages. Each timely motivational message contains three points for the viewers benefit that leaves them motivated and inspired. The message titles are:

1. Believe In Yourself (6 minutes)
2. The Power of Purpose (6 minutes)
3. Who Is Your Biggest Competitor (7 minutes)
4. Going The Extra Mile (7 minutes)
5. Focus On Your Successes (11 minutes)
6. Developing POSitive Expectations (7 minutes)

Most motivational videos are only good for one viewing. Not "MR POS", he delivers six messages which means no material is repeated until it is shown six times. What a great value and packaged all in one video!

POWER PACK

This combination has tremendous impact with any group. It consists of "MR POS's" six motivational messages, all on one video, along with 100 plastic GOLDEN ATTITUDE LAPEL PINS each attached to a card with his nine step definition of a GOLDEN ATTITUDE. You can begin today to empower your team members. Call us today to begin empowering your people tomorrow!

The Power Pack is a very cost effective way to begin building, or to reinforce existing POSitive attitudes in any company!
            Denise Hellebusch — D. D. Williamson Company

THE VIDEO-BASED EMPOWERMENT PROGRAM

A Total Empowerment Program
For Building POSitive Attitudes

This video based program from "MR POS" is designed to be delivered by anyone on your staff who has a desire to facilitate educational programs. It consists of four fifteen minute modules designed for your program facilitator to deliver the program with high impact using an easy to follow interactive handout. Each module in the handout can be presented separately or in a series with time spans ranging from 90 minutes to 4 hours. You get quality program facilitation as well as program flexibility.

To support the program facilitator, "MR POS" gives you ten points of POSitive facilitation as well as suggestions on how to facilitate each module. This video based program is the most complete program available and has been voted the most outstanding program with such companies as Ford Motor Company, Louisville Gas & Electric Company and the Internal Revenue Service.

This video based program is very cost effective and includes:

4 — Fifteen Minute Modules Entitled:
   Motivation — How do you empower it?
   Empowering POSitive Attitudes Toward Yourself
   Empowering POSitive Attitudes Toward Others
   Empowering POSitive Attitudes Toward Success
1 — Fifteen Minute "Facilitator Tips" Module
10 — Copies of "MR POS" #1 Best Selling Book
12 — Newsletter Articles
50 — Program Handouts
50 — Golden Attitude Lapel Pins
50 — Attitude Posters

Call for pricing information and a sample copy of the participant's handout.

Rich's program has allowed us to utilize the talents of our staff members as facilitators and empower attitudes of people within our school.
                              Mrs. Margaret Sellers — Assistant Principal

AUDIO CASSETTE SELF STUDY SYSTEM

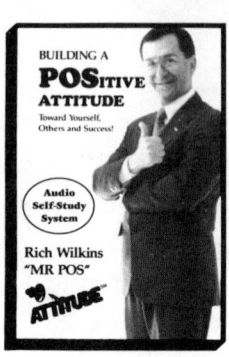

"Empowering POSitive Attitudes Toward
Yourself, Others and Success"

Several years of research have gone into this complete self study audio program! "MR POS" will introduce you to twelve powerful principles you can practice on a daily basis to POSitively empower yourself and others. Along with the principles, he will share many humorous stories that will raise your awareness levels of how to achieve more success in your personal, professional and spiritual lives. You will begin to discover more clearly how your values motivate you, how your past experiences have limited or propelled you into success, and why education and development are vital to your personal and professional growth.

You will also hear more about:

1. Building A POSitive Belief System
2. Focusing on your successes and learning from your failures
3. Surrounding yourself with POSitive successful people
4. The importance of faith
5. Seeing John Brown through John Brown's eyes
6. Don't compete with others, inspire them
7. Become a good finder in others
8. Going the extra mile
9. Having a life purpose
10. Overcoming failure
11. Serving others
12. Creative visualization

The complete system includes:
— 4 Audio Cassettes
— 1 Copy of Rich's Book
— 1 Copy of the Participant's Handout
— 1 Poster
— 1 Golden Attitude Lapel Pin

2 Additional ways to bring GOLDEN ATTITUDES to your office or home with our PLAQUES and POSTERS from
"MR POS"

ATTITUDE
by
Rich Wilkins

ATTITUDE isn't simply a state of mind . . . it is also a reflection of what we value. Attitude is more than just saying I can, it is believing you can. It requires believing before seeing, because seeing is based on circumstances, believing is based on faith. Attitude is so contagious especially when we allow it to turn our doubts of the past into passions of today and set the stage for our tomorrows. We have total ownership of our attitudes. No one else has the power to alter our attitudes without our permission. Our attitude allows us to become more empowering than money, to rise above our failures, and accept others for who they are, and what they say. It is more important than giftedness and is the forerunner of all skills needed for happiness and success. Our attitudes can be used to build us up or put us down - the choice is ours. It also gives us the wisdom to know that we can't change events of the past. I am convinced that life is 10% what happens to me, and 90% how I respond to it . . . and it is with this state of mind that I remain in charge of my ATTITUDES.

(PLAQUE #1)

A GOLDEN ATTITUDE IS...

Always making today your best day
Taking pride in a job well done
Treating others with respect
Isolating your negative thoughts
Treating every new task as an opportunity
Utilizing your talents daily
Doing the job right the first time
Expecting positive outcomes daily
Speaking well of others everyday

(PLAQUE #2)

Our attractive 9"X12" wooden plaques are available for only $22.50. The posters are 8.5"X11", have a high gloss white backround, gold foil lettering and are available for only $5. Should you order 10 plaques or posters you get one free! Mount them in;

* Company break rooms
* By the time clock
* Conference room
* Training room
* Customer service area
* Reception area

Should you want us to send one to a friend for you, simply call our office and we will take care of the details!

152 Rich Wilkins

Directions: Listed below you will see 24 groups of words describing style. In each group of 4 words select the word that best describes you. Place an X in the box in the MOST column for that word, then select a word that LEAST describes your style in that group. Place an X in the box next to that word in the least column.

Refer to example below before proceeding:

> **Example:**
> M L
> ☒ ☐ Gentle, kindly
> ☐ ☒ Persuasive, convincing
> ☐ ☐ Humble, reserved, modest
> ☐ ☐ Original, inventive, individualistic

NAME _____ COMPANY _____ MALE _____ FEMALE _____
FOCUS: WORK _____ HOME _____

M L

1.
- ☐ ☐ Gentle, kindly
- ☐ ☐ Persuasive, convincing
- ☐ ☐ Humble, reserved, modest
- ☐ ☐ Original, inventive, individualistic

2.
- ☐ ☐ Attractive, charming, attracts others
- ☐ ☐ Cooperative, agreeable
- ☐ ☐ Stubborn, unyielding
- ☐ ☐ Sweet, pleasing

3.
- ☐ ☐ Easily led, follower
- ☐ ☐ Bold, daring
- ☐ ☐ Loyal, faithful, devoted
- ☐ ☐ Charming, delightful

4.
- ☐ ☐ Open-minded, receptive
- ☐ ☐ Obliging, helpful
- ☐ ☐ Will power, strong willed
- ☐ ☐ Cheerful, joyful

5.
- ☐ ☐ Jovial, joking
- ☐ ☐ Precise, exact
- ☐ ☐ Nervy, gutsy, brazen
- ☐ ☐ Even-tempered, calm, not easily excited

6.
- ☐ ☐ Competitive, seeking to win
- ☐ ☐ Considerate, caring, thoughtful
- ☐ ☐ Outgoing, fun loving, socially striving
- ☐ ☐ Harmonious, agreeable

7.
- ☐ ☐ Fussy, hard to please
- ☐ ☐ Obedient, will do as told, dutiful
- ☐ ☐ Unconquerable, determined
- ☐ ☐ Playful, frisky, full of fun

8.
- ☐ ☐ Brave, unafraid, courageous
- ☐ ☐ Inspiring, stimulating, motivating
- ☐ ☐ Submissive, yielding, gives in
- ☐ ☐ Timid, shy, quiet

9.
- ☐ ☐ Sociable, enjoys company of others
- ☐ ☐ Patient, steady, tolerant
- ☐ ☐ Self-reliant, independent
- ☐ ☐ Soft-spoken, mild, reserved

10.
- ☐ ☐ Adventurous, willing to take chances
- ☐ ☐ Receptive, open to suggestions
- ☐ ☐ Cordial, warm, friendly
- ☐ ☐ Moderate, avoids extremes

11.
- ☐ ☐ Talkative, chatty
- ☐ ☐ Controlled, restrained
- ☐ ☐ Conventional, doing it the usual way, customary
- ☐ ☐ Decisive, certain, firm in making a decision

12.
- ☐ ☐ Polished, smooth talker
- ☐ ☐ Daring, risk-taker
- ☐ ☐ Diplomatic, tactful to people
- ☐ ☐ Satisfied, content, pleased

13.
- ☐ ☐ Aggressive, challenger, takes action
- ☐ ☐ Life of the party, outgoing, entertaining
- ☐ ☐ Easy mark, easily taken advantage of
- ☐ ☐ Fearful, afraid

14.
- ☐ ☐ Cautious, wary, careful
- ☐ ☐ Determined, decided, unwavering, stand firm
- ☐ ☐ Convincing, assuring
- ☐ ☐ Good-natured, pleasant

15.
- ☐ ☐ Willing, go along with
- ☐ ☐ Eager, anxious
- ☐ ☐ Agreeable, consenting
- ☐ ☐ High-spirited, lively, enthusiastic

16.
- ☐ ☐ Confident, believes in self, assured
- ☐ ☐ Sympathetic, compassionate, understanding
- ☐ ☐ Tolerant
- ☐ ☐ Assertive, aggressive

17.
- ☐ ☐ Well-disciplined, self-controlled
- ☐ ☐ Generous, willing to share
- ☐ ☐ Animated, uses gestures for expression
- ☐ ☐ Persistent, unrelenting, refuses to quit

18.
- ☐ ☐ Admirable, deserving of praise
- ☐ ☐ Kind, willing to give or help
- ☐ ☐ Resigned, gives in
- ☐ ☐ Force of character, powerful

19.
- ☐ ☐ Respectful, shows respect
- ☐ ☐ Pioneering, exploring, enterprising
- ☐ ☐ Optimistic, positive view
- ☐ ☐ Accommodating, willing to please, ready to help

20.
- ☐ ☐ Argumentative, confronting
- ☐ ☐ Adaptable, flexible
- ☐ ☐ Nonchalant, casually indifferent
- ☐ ☐ Light-hearted, carefree

21.
- ☐ ☐ Trusting, faith in others
- ☐ ☐ Contented, satisfied
- ☐ ☐ Positive, admitting no doubt
- ☐ ☐ Peaceful, tranquil

22.
- ☐ ☐ Good mixer, likes being with others
- ☐ ☐ Cultured, educated, knowledgeable
- ☐ ☐ Vigorous, energetic
- ☐ ☐ Lenient, not overly strict, tolerant of others' actions

23.
- ☐ ☐ Companionable, easy to be with
- ☐ ☐ Accurate, correct
- ☐ ☐ Outspoken, speaks freely and boldly
- ☐ ☐ Restrained, reserved, controlled

24.
- ☐ ☐ Restless, unable to rest or relax
- ☐ ☐ Neighborly, friendly
- ☐ ☐ Popular, liked by many or most people
- ☐ ☐ Orderly, neat, organized

Printed by permission of Target Training International, Ltd.

CHAPTER 12
WORKSHOP INFORMATION

Looking for a Speaker that Makes a POSitive Difference!

"MR POS" will take you back to the basics to create POSitive attitudes about your people, their potential and opportunities for success! He will build exciting new energy in any company or organization by helping people develop a more POSitive outlook. It's the first step in any successful training or motivational program, especially if your company is experiencing change!

Rich has worked for many companies. He has conduted programs for Ford Motor Company, Merrill Lynch, IBM Corporation, Internal Revenue Services, Citibank, State Farm Insurance Companies and Holiday Inns of America plus many more. In 1990, he was voted most outstanding independent trainer by the partcipants at Ford Motor Company. By developing clear purpose for his company, accepting failure as a stepping stone to success and placing himself in a serving role to others, he has realized tremendous business growth. Prior to starting his own company he served others through professional sales, management and corporate training. He is the past director of the University of Louisville Sales School, is active in the National Speaker's Association and is an Area Governor for Toastmasters International. Rich is a firm believer that one's ATTITUDE is not just a state of mind, it is also a reflection of one's values.

KEYNOTE SPEECHES

Rich conducts many keynote presentations each year to companies and associations (large and small). He conducts breakfast, luncheon and dinner keynotes inspiring the audiences by getting them involved in his presentations.

Rich's presentations are excellent for "kicking off" any meeting or for ending it on a very inspirational and POSitive note.

KEYNOTE PRESENTATION TITLE:
"Empowering POSitive Attitudes Toward Yourself, Others and Success"

PRESENTATION OBJECTIVES:
1. Give the audience an inspirational message about human potential.
2. Understand the power of purpose.
3. Understand how failing events are a part of the success process.
4. Understanding that success comes through serving others.

FORMAT:
Thirty to forty minutes in length. This keynote involves the audience with high enery levels.

AUDIO VISUAL REQUIREMENTS:
Flip chart for groups of less than 100, overhead projector for larger groups.

WORKSHOP PRESENTATIONS

Empowering Attitudes

WORKSHOP TITLE:
"Empowering POSitive Attitudes Toward Yourself, Others and Success"

WORKSHOP OBJECTIVES:
1. Deliver an inspirational workshop for all participants.
2. Raise awareness levels of all participants toward themselves, others and success.
3. Cover twelve proven principles to build attitudes toward themselves and others.
4. Determine who limits us more than anyone else and why.
5. Learn how to use POSitive self-talk to create a POSitive life style.
6. Learn how behavior and values impact motivation.

NOTE:
Our workshops will be customized to meet the needs of your company, association or industry. This workshop is especially beneficial to companies in transition and change.

FORMAT:
Two Hour Sessions. The above workshop can be expanded to one half day and full day workshops with additional training materials added.

AUDIO VISUAL REQUIREMENTS:
Groups of 100 or less, flip chart, VCR and monitor.
Groups of over 100 an overhead projector.

ROOM SET-UP:
Classroom or theater style seating.

MATERIALS:
A professionally published master copy of a handout is provided for you to photocopy for all participants.

MISCELLANEOUS INFORMATION:
1. At the time a decision is made to contract my speaking/training services a 20% deposit is required.
2. The client will provide all meeting facilities and audio visual equipment.
3. The above fees do not include travel, lodging and meals.
4. Any portion of the training can be audio or video recorded at no additional fee to the client.
5. Rich Wilkins & Company would appreciate your written recommendation of his speaking/training services to three business associates upon your complete satisfaction and approval of his program.

All keynote presentations and workshops are conducted with high energy levels and are audience participative. We believe all educational training should be fun and "content based" in which the participants feel inspired and have principles to apply in their daily living.

As a prospective client, you may want to contact others who have utilized my services. Please feel free to contact these valued clients:

Connie Renfro –	Internal Revenue Service	502-582-5377
Estelle Andrews –	Citibank, Inc.	415-891-8974
Mindy Morrow –	Atlas Van Lines, Inc.	800-638-9797
Kathy Smith –	Ford Motor Company	502-364-3509
Brian Kramer –	IBM Corporation	404-980-3321
Susan Newkirk-Moore –	KY Bankers Association	502-582-2453

Rich's programs are a must for any company experiencing change. We utilized his services at our Ford Explorer Plant in Louisville with very positive results.

Kathy Smith, Training – Ford Motor Company

SALES WORKSHOPS

Empowering Your Selling Skills

Selling professionally is a process! It is not doing something to someone, but doing something with and for people that is "needs driven," "values focused," has integrity, and is mutually beneficial. I have a philosophy about selling that is based on this principle;

"If you can see John Brown through John Brown's eyes, you can sell John Brown what John Brown buys."

Too many sales people want to present products and services before they try to understand their prospect's needs. Before we can create value for John Brown we must take the time to listen and determine his needs. My sales programs do just that by helping sales people understand what is important to the prospect to give added value.

Rich's program is a process which begins with building salespeople's self-confidence and helps them understand the selling process in total. It has the greatest impact when conducted over a period of time. Each session is approximately two hours in length and the session titles are as follows:

1. Empowering Selling Attitudes
2. Empowering Buyer/Seller Relationships
3. Empowering Time & Territory Management
4. Empowering Needs Assessment Selling
5. Empowering Your Sales Presentation
6. Empowering Mutual Commitment (Closing)

Rich is the past director of the University of Louisville Sales School and has trained thousands of sales people. Please feel free to contact the following clients in regard to the effectiveness of his sales development series:

Dave Caudill –	Pride, Inc.	502-585-1325
Jim Lintner –	CompDent, Inc.	502-456-1800
Mindy Morrow –	Atlas Van Lines	800-638-9797
Sheleen Fryer –	Blue Cross/Blue Shield	502-423-2099
Jean Bright –	The Future Now	502-495-2500

Professional sales people never close a sale, they simply continue to build long term profitable sales relationships.

Rich "MR POS" Wilkins

PROFESSIONAL IMAGE WORKSHOPS

Karyn Pfeiffer, an image consultant for corporate America for the past ten years has put together a program she developed three years ago that offers an informative and entertaining presentation of the do's and don'ts of business and professional etiquette and protocol.

Her two-hour professional image makers seminar includes:

- The Professional Etiquette Quiz
- The Anatomy Of A Handshake
- The Business Of A Business Card
- An Introduction To Introducing
- The Business Lunch and Dinner

Karyn's program is designed to polish any professional and enhance the total image of any company.

Karyn is currently working on a book entitled Recipes For A Professional Image. Karyn lives in Louisville, Kentucky, with her husband, Mark, a local news anchorman. They have one son, A.J.

ORDER FORM

Quantity Ordered	Item	Price Each	Amount
	"Classic" Attitude Pin (pg 146)	$ 5.00	
	Plastic Attitude Pin (pg 147)	$ 2.00	
	Book	$ 9.95	
	Video #1 (pg 148)	$ 79.95	
	Power Pack (pg 148)	$285.00	
	Audio Program (pg 150)	$ 49.95	
	Posters (pg 151)	$ 5.00	
	Plaque (pg 151)	$ 22.50	
	Other		
	SUB-TOTAL		
	SHIPPING (PINS, POSTERS, BOOKS)	$ 5.00	
	SALES TAX (KY RESIDENTS ONLY)		
	TOTAL ENCLOSED		

For larger orders of books and plaques call our office for shipping charges.

☐ Check or money order enclosed.   Amount $ _____
☐ MasterCard   ☐ VISA   ☐ Amer. Exp.   Amount $ _____
Account No. _____ Exp. Date _____
Cardholder Signature _____

Please send the items listed to:
Name _____
Company Name _____
Street Address _____
City _____ State _____ Zip _____
Telephone _____

You Can Fax Your Order to: 502-955-9795 — OR

Mail To:
Rich Wilkins & Company
4817 Running Fox Drive
Shepherdsville, KY 40165

For More Information,
Please Call:
Rich Wilkins & Company
502-955-7269 Office

Rich Wilkins